When the Spirits Come Back

Marie-Louise von Franz, Honorary Patron

**Studies in Jungian Psychology
by Jungian Analysts**

Daryl Sharp, General Editor

When the Spirits Come Back

JANET O. DALLETT

I thank the patients who have lent themselves so generously
to this work.

I thank the Writer's Group: David Mathieson, Carolyn
Latteier, Alex Fowler, Ru Kirk and Nick Dallett.

Some of the royalties for this book will go to Tamanawas,
an interest-free loan fund for people in breakdown who
seek nontraditional treatment.

Canadian Cataloguing in Publication Data

Dallett, Janet O. (Osborn), 1933-
 When the spirits come back

(Studies in Jungian psychology by Jungian analysts; 33)

Includes bibliographical references.
ISBN 0-919123-32-5

1. Dallett, Janet.   2. Psychoanalysis.
3. Jung, C.G. (Carl Gustav), 1875-1961.
I. Title.   II. Series.

BF173.D34 1988   150.19'54'0924   C88-093728-9

INNER CITY BOOKS
Box 1271, Station Q, Toronto, Canada M4T 2P4
Telephone (416) 927-0355

Honorary Patron: Marie-Louise von Franz.
Publisher and General Editor: Daryl Sharp.
Editor: Vicki Cowan.
Editorial Board: Fraser Boa, Daryl Sharp, Marion Woodman.
Production and Marketing: Ben Sharp, David Sharp.

INNER CITY BOOKS was founded in 1980 to promote the
understanding and practical application of the work of C.G. Jung.

Cover painting by Canadian artist Anne B. Knoop

Printed and bound in Canada by Webcom Limited

Contents

See final pages for descriptions of other Inner City Books

Acknowledgments

Chapter 1, "Foundations of Madness," appeared in *Whole Earth Review,* spring 1988.

An earlier version of chapter 2, "Shaman, Artist, Lunatic, Thief," appeared in *Psychological Perspectives,* spring 1986.

Portions of chapter 8, "A Time for Thieves," appeared in *Whole Earth Review,* winter 1986; reprinted in *Free Spirit,* May-June 1987.

Chapter 10, "When the Spirits Come Back," appeared in *Whole Earth Review,* Spring 1986; reprinted in *Free Spirit* and in *The Message.* A longer version is in the fall 1985/winter 1986 double issue of *Voices: The Art and Science of Psychotherapy,* reprinted in book form as *Carl Jung and Soul Psychology,* ed. Gibson, Lathrop and Stern (New York: The Haworth Press, 1986.)

CW in the footnotes refers to *The Collected Works of C.G. Jung* (Bollingen Series XX), 20 vols., trans. R.F.C. Hull, ed. H. Read, M. Fordham, G. Adler, Wm. McGuire (Princeton: Princeton University Press, 1953-1979).

The voice of thy brother's blood
crieth unto me from the ground.
                    —Genesis 4:10.

Preface

Where I grew up, one of the worst sins for a woman was not to feed the guests in her house. No one actually said the words, but they might as well have been lettered on a sign and posted in the kitchen along with other unspoken imperatives:

BEWARE OF AUNT LILLIAN,
THE NEW YORK ACTRESS!
SEX? YECH!
PLEASE BE NICE.
TELL THE TRUTH AT YOUR PERIL.
FEED YOUR GUESTS, WOMAN!

These things die hard. All last month I searched my psyche for more food to give you who read this book. I tried to explain why I have brought this material together under one cover and to give you the definitive word about what it says. I struggled to tell you how to think and feel about it to insure that you would be fully satisfied and not go away hungry.

My hands grew clammy and I clutched the pencil tighter when I recalled the words of an editor who had read the manuscript:

"I don't want to lay a patriarchal trip on you," he said. "I *love* this book! But let me tell you the cold hard facts of the marketplace. These days you can't sell a book that doesn't fit into one of the accepted categories. Before we contract for a book, we have to be able to tell the book dealer what shelf it belongs on in his store."

Several dozen editors and an agent agreed.

I turned myself inside out to fit my writing into a category. In despair, I looked up the word *category* in the dictionary and found that one of its meanings is "predicament." The prefix *cat-* means "against," and *-agora* is the marketplace.

9

Wait a minute, I thought. If *category* is against the marketplace, how can it be that nothing will sell without a category? I'm getting into a predicament. Everything is backward.

Then I had a dream:

"A crowd has begun to gather for some event at my house. It is decided that everyone will stay for dinner. I am concerned because I do not think I have enough food for so many people, but they say not to worry. They will take care of it.

"We all sit down to dinner at several long tables. The people have collected all the food in the house and created a rich cornbread from it. That is the whole dinner. At first I think more will be required, but when I taste the cornbread I know it will be enough. It contains so many things that it is a satisfying meal in itself."

Cornbread is made from the native American grain. Where I come from, it is soul food. Welcome to my house. Enjoy your meal!

1

Foundations of Madness

"Spit in your shoe and you'll go to Kalamazoo."

I removed my six-year-old eyes from the mail slot and stared at Jo Ann. The fate of the three small stones we had mailed no longer mattered. Seeing the power of her incantation, she began to chant it over and over in a high, singsong voice, "SPIT in your SHOE and you'll GO to KalamaZOO!"

I began to giggle at the sound of the words and the vision they evoked: a zoo full of wondrous beasts sitting like people with their shoes off, spitting in them. Jo Ann giggled too, and fell to the ground. Rolling back and forth in the springtime grass, we shrieked with laughter and hugged our chests so it wouldn't hurt so much.

A long time later I understood the intolerance and thoughtless cruelty hidden behind the silly saying, repeated again and again in the small Michigan farming community of my childhood. The state mental hospital was in Kalamazoo, thirty miles away. If you did anything too unusual, you might be locked up with the other crazy people there. That was a problem for me because I could not seem to learn to do things right. My mother kept saying, "If you're not nicer to people, they're not going to like you." I knew it meant I should do things the way she did. God knows I tried. When people I had no use for came to visit, I would dutifully put down the book I was reading and do my best to make polite, phony conversation like my mother's, but I had no gift for it. As a result I made the adults uncomfortable. They were always saying, "What's the matter? Cat got your tongue?"

Later, after I got a scholarship to go to the liberal arts college on the *other* hill in Kalamazoo, it was Gene, my first sweetheart, who landed in the mental hospital. He and I used to sneak into the college chapel, take our clothes off and pet in the tiny basement room where the Founder was buried underneath the floor. Gene, a son of fundamentalist Christian parents, had qualms about it. I felt a little queasy myself, more about the Founder than the sex, so I helped him comb the Bible for comforting words that would justify what we had done already and wanted to do again.

The harder we looked, the more elusive were the words we hoped to find. I came across 1 Corinthians 13 and began to read it to Gene:

"If I speak in the tongues of men and of angels, but have not love, I am a noisy gong or a clanging cymbal. And if I have prophetic poses, and understand all mysteries and all knowledge, and if I have all faith, so as to move mountains, but have not love, I am nothing. . . ."

His attention was riveted. I went on to the end of the chapter:

". . . So faith, hope, love abide, these three; but the greatest of these is love."[1]

For days we wrestled with the words, trying desperately to grasp the depths of their intent. Then Gene fell into the hands of the living God. He struggled with myriad inner voices, at odds with one another and most of all with the narrow values that had formed him. The spiritual sensibility of an earlier time might have seen in his torment the mark of a healer or holy man, and honored it. I saw the man I loved searching for his soul. Middle America in the 1950s saw only insanity.

Childhood came to a shattering end. They warned me that Gene would hurt me, but I knew he would not, and walked all night alone with him anyway. I remember frantic nights fading into frantic days, rivers of blood that would not stop when tension broke an artery in my nose, an inexplicably angry nurse and a night in the college infirmary. I remember Gene's white face against a hospital pillow, his voice saying, "I'm sorry, Janet," before he disappeared into an unseen world. I remember the day he was locked up in the mental hospital on the other hill, visitors forbidden. When I was allowed to see him after several weeks, a rational but spiritless stranger occupied his

---

[1] Revised Standard Version.

body. I now suppose he had been given electroshock to save him from the dark night of his soul. Then I supposed nothing.

Having glimpsed my own soul's face in the mirror of Gene's madness, I grieved my loss endlessly. My heart knew that a terrible crime had occurred. Years later, when I heard of his physical death, I was bewildered. To me he had been murdered long before.

Gradually my loyalties shifted. By the time I was forty, I understood why some of the people society calls crazy get locked up. They see too much.

I lived in Los Angeles then, and was an analyst-in-training at the C.G. Jung Institute. A brand new doctoral degree hung over my head like Damocles' sword. In graduate school I had learned to be a Professional Person and to maintain my authority by keeping clear boundaries between myself and my patients. Every morning I got up and put on a face designed to make an appropriate impression. One day I dressed in a tasteful red suit with a clean white blouse and navy blue pumps and went to meet a new patient who, I was told, was schizophrenic.

Barbara said she had trouble waking up in the morning. "Some days I can't get out of bed at all," she told me. Then she looked me straight in the eye. "Why, I can't even get it together enough to dress up like a flag in red white and blue."

I wish I could say I laughed, but I did not. I recoiled. Barbara kindly waited for me to recover, and we went on as if nothing had happened. Later, as the hour drew to an end, she observed, "You're in a very dangerous profession, you know." I was beginning to see what she meant. My professional authority was in a shambles. Barbara touched parts of myself I had never seen before and did not want to know. I felt like telling her, "If you're not nicer, people won't like you." The more she talked, the more convinced I became that she was too crazy to be running around loose. If I could put her in a mental hospital, I would feel safe from her. Safe from myself.

My reaction was typical. Crazy people strip us of defenses and confront us with truths we would prefer to avoid. We hospitalize and drug them beyond recognition because we are afraid of what they activate in us, not because it will help them. Everyone goes a little crazy in the presence of insanity. If we were willing to acknowledge and suffer the madness in ourselves, we could participate in its healing, but it is infinitely easier to make scapegoats of those who have been overwhelmed by it.

The God of the Old Testament gives careful instructions for scapegoating:

"Aaron must lay his hands on [the head of a living goat] and confess all the faults of the sons of Israel, all their transgressions and all their sins, and lay them to its charge. Having thus laid them on the goat's head, he shall send it out into the desert led by a man waiting ready, and the goat will bear all their faults away with it into a desert place."[2]

Barbara did not become my scapegoat. I learned to let her play a different role in my life, mocking my pretensions like a court jester or a Native American clown.

In *Daughters of Copper Woman*,[3] Anne Cameron describes the practice of clowning through the eyes of Granny, an old Nootka woman:

"If you thought every word you spoke was gospel, the clown would just stroll along behind you babblin' away like a simple-mind or a baby. Every up and down of your voice, the clown's voice would go up and down until you finally heard what an ass you were bein'. Or maybe you had a bad temper and yelled a lot when you got mad, or hadn't learned any self control or somethin' like that. Well, the clown would just have fits. Every time you turned around there'd be the clown bashin' away with a stick on the sand or kickin' like a fool at a big rock, or yellin' insults back at the gulls, and just generally lookin' real stupid.

"We needed our clowns, and we used 'em to help us all learn the best ways to get along with each other. Bein' an individual is real

---

[2] Leviticus 16:21-22, Jerusalem Bible.
[3] Vancouver, BC: Press Gang Publishers, 1981.

good, but sometimes we're so busy bein' individuals we forget we gotta live with a lot of other people who all got the right to be individuals too, and the clowns could show us if we were gettin' a bit pushy, or startin' to take ourselves too serious."

It occurred to me one day that if I could learn to see people as clearly as Barbara did in her presumed insanity, I would become a very good therapist indeed. As time went on and her gentle ridicule put my self-importance in perspective, I saw that she was doing at least as much for me as I for her. I began to question the extravagant notion that therapists heal their patients. A heretical thought lodged in my head and throbbed like a sore tooth: Perhaps when people stop acting crazy, it has nothing to do with the power of psychotherapists. Maybe our knowledge, our skills and technical achievements are beside the point.

I remembered a story a psychology student at Berkeley told me in the late 1950s, when psychotropic drugs were first being tested. At the mental hospital where she worked, a long-term chronic psychotic named George was picked to ingest an experimental dose of thorazine every day. No one had paid George any attention for years. Now doctors, attendants and nurses all talked to him and watched eagerly to see what effect the drug would have. His condition improved rapidly. After only two weeks of the drug treatment, he was moved to a ward for less disturbed patients, where he took part in a number of activities. Soon he was doing so well that he was promoted again. By this time he had lively relationships with the other patients and many members of the hospital staff. He began to spend several hours a day with paints and clay, using them to express the rich fantasy life that had previously interested no one. His doctors marveled. Attendants praised his skill.

George was released from the hospital thirty-eight days after his first dose of thorazine. While he was signing out, he remembered that he had left something behind, went back to his room, and returned with an old sock. The puzzled attendant who asked to see it found thirty-eight thorazine pills carefully stashed inside the sock.

Why, then, had George suddenly come to life?

Thirty years later I was still asking questions. My psychologist friend Rosemary was annoyed with me. "Don't you know you have to play the game? You can't say what you really think. Sometimes you just have to tell people what they want to hear. Haven't you learned that yet?"

It was the third time I had heard it that week. My mother's voice echoed and re-echoed, "If you're not nicer to people, they're not going to like you," but I was fifty-four years old, my mother long since dead, and I had just failed one of my profession's major initiation rituals, the oral examination for state licensure.

"Are initiations *only* ordeals?" I wondered. "Aren't they supposed to be meaningful?" I smiled to placate Rosemary, and shrugged. I was thinking about the suit.

Two weeks before the exam I had said to myself, "Janet, you don't look right. What you need is a suit." The next day I took the ferry to Seattle and tried on suits, maybe fifty of them. No matter what I put on, I *still* didn't look right.

Exhausted, I stared at my aging, slip-clad body in Nordstrom's mirror and contemplated half a century of examinations, from grade school to high school, college and graduate school, through five years of specialized analytic training and licensure in another state. "I think I've gotten too old to play the game any more," I thought. "I'll have to be myself. No suit."

"You're *what?*" said Rosemary. "You're going to go as *yourself?!* Jesus! That's professional suicide."

As soon as I entered the examination room, one of the men looked me from toe to head, taking in every detail of my comfortable flat-heeled boots, stylish black cotton skirt, green L.L. Bean sweater, authentic Native American trade beads, and undisciplined baby-fine hair. His lip curled just enough to show his opinion before he turned to introduce me to the chairman, an imposing woman dressed in a suit.

In response to her first question, I began to discuss my work with a suicidal patient who had had a breakdown. Recently I had come to the radical conclusion that breakdown is the first step in a natural healing process. I knew it would not be wise to talk about that, so I tried instead to describe my first three hours with the patient.

When I looked at the lip curler, he didn't bother to cover his yawn. The other man coughed. The chairman shuffled her feet a few times and finally interrupted me. "Can you formulate her problem in a . . . in a . . . briefly? Why she felt suicidal and why she became psychotic?"

"In a nutshell?" I thought. "God forbid that you should say nutshell and make us all laugh. God forbid that you should let us be human. . . . Sure. No problem. Just formulate why she went crazy in a few well-chosen sentences."

The silence was getting too long. I felt naked. My ears rang and my radical ideas pulled at me like a magnet. I looked down at the table in front of me and sighed. Slowly and awkwardly I began to speak:

"Well . . . I have a theory about psychosis. My sense is that people often become psychotic because they have constructed a personality that is not congruent with who they really are. This happens because they are sensitive children who perceive things going on in their environment that are not confirmed by the people around them, like their parents. For instance, they may perceive the hidden emotions in the family, but when they act on what they see, or speak of it, the parents deny that those emotions are present. So the child builds up a personality for the sake of adaptation that is quite incongruent with his or her true nature. As life goes on, this discrepancy between the adaptation and the real person becomes greater and greater, so that a rather large split develops. Often in psychosis what happens is that the true personality . . . it looks to me as if this true personality begins to reach out and demand to be seen and heard, and it eventually overwhelms the ego and simply takes over. It's as if the ego dissolves—an ego that is brittle and not connected in a human way to what the person *is* deeply. So it seems to me that this kind of psychotic episode is an opportunity for the person to heal in a deeper way and to restore . . ."

The chairman cleared her throat. I stopped talking and looked at her. Her mouth was opening and closing like a fish's. Her eyes rolled wildly. I waited, my anxiety level rising. There was an edge to her voice when she finally spoke. "Are you familiar with any other kinds of theories of personality besides . . . ahh . . . the one from which you work?"

I was startled. Hadn't they looked at my transcripts? "Well . . . I majored in personality when I was at UCLA, so . . ."

"Would you be able to formulate your case in terms of another . . . a very different theory than the one that you are using? Say . . . behaviorism?"

Behaviorism is probably the most influential of the dozens of theories currently applied to psychotherapeutic methods. It rests on what is known as the "empty organism" point of view which assumes, for theoretical purposes, that nothing of importance happens inside a person. All that matters is what goes in (stimulus) and what comes out (response). Behaviorism denies the existence of unconscious processes and has no interest in dreams. Even conscious thoughts, feelings, intuitions or sensations are considered to be of no consequence.

My head spun. I saw an abyss as vast as the Grand Canyon open in front of me, my examiners receding into the distance at the far rim. I remembered a conversation I once had with a behaviorist professor at Berkeley. When I told him I had been thinking about something, he snapped at me, "I don't know what that word 'think' means!" I had dared not give voice to my sassy internal response: "It's one of those things you can't understand unless you've done it."

I looked at the chairman. Formulate my patient's problem in terms of behaviorism? "No, I don't think I can do that," I said, signing my death warrant.

Half an hour later, I left. I would not hear the official results for several weeks, but I knew. Maybe I would take the exam again, I thought. Maybe I could disguise myself and play the game, one more time.

My mind went to Kent, my one-time husband and soulmate. I remembered the baby squids that he liked to cook whole, staring up at me from the plate, and how he used to tell his psychology students not to go to medical school because it would ruin their minds. I remembered my mother disliking him because he picked his nose in public, and how she hated his favorite song about the cannibal boy who says to his parents, "Don't eat people, eating people is wrong!" while the parents indignantly defend their lifestyle by telling him that "people have always eaten people."

I remembered his years of black depression, the day of the divorce neither of us really wanted, and the midnight phone call, six years later, bringing the news of his suicide. I imagine he was too tired of his role to go on with it. Sickness or death are often the only excuses our culture accepts from someone who can't, or won't, play the game. It is not enough to say no.

While he was alive, I don't know that Kent made a conscious effort to expose hypocrisy, but things did have a way of rolling over and showing their underbelly in his presence. Merchants all over West Los Angeles grew to dread his approach, because he had only to look at a piece of goods whose shoddiness was concealed beneath a pretty exterior for it to fall apart. Hoping to help his career, I once invited some graduate students to dinner, along with the department chairman and his wife. Our small grey cat Synchronicity was in heat. As we sat in a stiff little circle in the living room, making proper pre-dinner conversation, the cat ran into the house at top speed, pursued by an ardent lover, and consummated her relationship smack in the midst of us. That's how it was with Kent. His genius for authenticity would not be subverted.

Kent and I divided the labor in our marriage. He was the enfant terrible, leaving me free to be the nice young faculty wife who fit in and made a good impression. It was only after his death that the dissidence in my own nature began to come back to me.

Sometimes I have the feeling that there is a place in the psyche, way down deep, where all of us are dreaming the same dream. Jung named it the collective unconscious. Whoever dives to that level comes back with stories that native people call big dreams, recognizing that they belong to the whole tribe. Some go there in sleep, some in visions or other altered states of consciousness. People who know how to go to the place of the big dream and bring back healing for themselves and others are called shamans.

Our culture has no niche for people who descend to the place of the big dream. Unless they happen to be artists, they have no place to take their gifts, and they risk being thought crazy if they speak of what they see. If they do not speak of it, they may in fact go crazy from carrying alone a burden of symbolic material that belongs to the culture as a whole, material that could heal our social wounds if we received and understood it.

Certain times in the life of the individual are like windows into the place of the big dream, revealing glimpses of mysterious threads that bind our destinies one to the other and make meaningful patterns in our lives. Although the Western scientific mind finds it difficult to grasp, Eastern thought takes for granted that everything happening at a given moment is connected. For example, the Chinese I Ching is based on the belief that if I am in tune with the universe, my toss of three coins will yield a hexagram whose meaning will be of a piece with my personal dilemma at this time. It is as if every slice of time is marked by a pattern different from that of other slices. People born during the depression have psychological traits in common that distinguish them from baby boomers. Music of the 1960s is recognizably different from that of the 40s. Because the coincidence in time of meaningfully related events often cannot be explained by the laws of cause and effect, Jung proposed that a different law governs such occurrences. He named it synchronicity.

A time of extraordinary synchronicity came to me after the license exam. For almost a week I felt numb, as if I were in a state of shock. Then I dreamed that someone had been murdered. Although I had not personally committed the murder, I was connected with the group responsible for it. The evidence was in my computer, and I felt unbearably guilty.

Waking, I questioned myself about the dream. How much do I participate in the murderousness of the culture to which I belong? Is the dream connected with the license exam? If I try to play the game and join the group, will I add moral weight to treatment methods I see as killers? Am I the murdered one? The murderer? Why *now,* at just this time, do I have to reclaim my piece of the murderer that exists as a potential in everyone and confront the problem of collective guilt?

I thought about Cain, the original murderer in the Judeo-Christian psyche. God respected the offering that Abel brought him, but spurned his brother Cain's. Cain was so angry that he murdered Abel, and when God asked where Abel was, Cain denied responsibility, saying, "Am I my brother's keeper?"[4]

Humiliation is a dangerous thing. If I were not careful, my reaction to failure would make a killer of me, just as the rage of powerlessness made Cain kill Abel and drives many an abused child to become an abusive adult. Then, too, therapists are given almost unlimited influence over the lives of others. I have to remind myself again and again that it is not I who heal my patients, but when I relate to them honestly, focusing attention on the mysterious forces that have more power to effect change than what I know consciously, something healing is born between us. When I forget, I become a little Hitler and try to create my patients in my own or society's image of who they should be. Then I am a murderer.

Later that same day I called my son Nick. Almost as soon as he picked up the telephone he said, "I had a really weird experience a little while ago while I was having a massage. I had a series of vivid visions. At the beginning, I was lying in a hospital. My body was shattered, as if I had had a terrible accident. I was waiting to die. Then there was a scene in a house at Morgan Beach, and at the end I was in Dad's old apartment. The one where he lived when he killed himself."

---

4 Genesis 4:4-9, King James Version.

My stomach lurched the way it always does when Nick gives me a glimpse of where he lives inside, but I only asked, "What's for you in Morgan Beach?"

"Not much," he said. "The last time I was in LA, I went there to give Erika Hauptmann a massage."

My mind was blank. I had lost track of Erika several years earlier, and I had no inkling why Nick should have such a terrible vision just now.

The telephone awakened me before dawn the next day. I recognized the voice of a colleague in Southern California, a member of the professional group I had left several years before. "Janet," she said, "has anyone called you about Erika?"

"What? Erika who?"

"Hauptmann. She jumped from a second-story window and died yesterday morning. I thought you'd want to know."

"God! What happened?"

"No one knows. There was no note. I'm afraid it wasn't a surprise, though. She'd been pretty crazy for a while. She was on medication for depression, but it only seemed to make it worse. There were some hallucinations. And she was still having nightmares about the Nazis."

A dull pain settled in my chest. As soon as I could, I ended the conversation. In the years I had known her, Erika had never been crazy. In pain, yes, but living with it. We had not been close friends, and I wondered why the news affected me so badly. Then I remembered Nick's vision and my dream. Somehow, in that place where we all dream the same dream, we were involved.

If anyone knew about collective guilt, Erika did. Born in Germany in the 1920s, she lived her late childhood and early adolescence during the Third Reich. She was forced to avoid her Jewish friends, who gradually disappeared from school and the neighborhood, one by one. Although the very air she breathed belonged to Hitler, her vulnerable young psyche still perceived that something terrible was happening. She voiced her objections and increasingly won the disapproval of peers, teachers and family, until fear and ostracism finally silenced her.

Even after she immigrated to the United States, Erika carried an intolerable burden of guilt, an irrational but unshakeable sense of responsibility for the Nazi murders. Bearing the load that others, less sensitive than she, had long ago shed, she struggled year by year to come to terms with the Nazi invasion that pursued her in her dreams. When it erupted into her daytime consciousness in the form of paranoid delusions and hallucinations, she finally became as fully its victim as if she had been a Jew.

I first met Erika when she was in graduate school, one of Kent's students at UCLA. In fact, she was there when Synchronicity the cat met her lover in the middle of my dinner party. I didn't see her again until she entered the analyst training program at the Jung Institute, fifteen years later. In the interval, Kent and I had had a child and divorced, I had become an analyst, and Kent had died. Four years after that, Erika asked me to supervise the final phase of her training. Only then, as her control analyst, did I learn something of her personal story and touch the psychological pain with which she lived, pain hidden behind the masks that we imagined were appropriate to the context of our earlier meetings.

When I moved to Seal Harbor, Washington, Erika visited me for a few more hours of consultation. She fell in love with Seal Harbor and made plans to retire there. Then she returned to Los Angeles and passed her final examination at the Jung Institute. Some time after that she went crazy. I did not hear from her again in this life. In the place of the big dream I must have known her well, for when she died, my inner killer came home.

The English language has almost as many labels for crazy people as Eskimos have for different kinds of snow. Insane, mad, nuts, maniac, lunatic, psychotic, schizophrenic, paranoid, manic-depressive. . . . Such words isolate madness from its context by locating it cleanly within the individual. How easy it then is to separate ourselves from someone's breakdown!

There is a Hopi word I like better. *Koyaanisqatsi* means:

1. crazy life
2. life in turmoil
3. life disintegrating
4. life out of balance
5. state of life calling for another way of living

2

Shaman, Artist, Lunatic, Thief

My father, a closet homosexual, abandoned both his sexuality and his creativity in 1919 when he came home from The War, married my mother, and never returned to Ann Arbor and the architectural career for which he had been destined.

I suppose I should be grateful that his self-desertion made an opportunity for my birth, but it has been a mixed blessing. I was thrust into the world during a blizzard on the day the banks closed, at the nadir of the Great Depression, and ever after it was implied that I might have had the grace to remain behind in my mother's mid-life womb, making it possible for my father to become the equal of Frank Lloyd Wright. Instead, he despaired his life away at a small factory job to support the children of whom I was third and last.

Like all parents who beg the question of their own destiny and sacrifice too much "for the sake of the children," my father passed his problems along to me unchanged. His life did not transform the dilemma of creativity one iota. Had he been able to relate to the woman within him, she might have redeemed him, but my father was a man of his time and felt he had no choice but to suppress her. Given no other voice, she became a petty tyrant of whose domination he was as much victim as we. Every morning at breakfast, my father silently wept. No one ever asked him what was the matter. No one dared. By then she had terrorized us all.

I was four years old the time my mother talked back to my father and refused to cook his dinner. He announced that the judge who lived next door would order her to cook the meal to which his conjugal rights entitled him. While he went to see the judge, my mother took me down town and spent ten cents on a double-dip lemon custard ice-cream cone. It was still Depression time and dimes were scarce. I felt so guilty about having all that money and attention lav-

25

ished on me that I tripped and spilled the ice cream right outside the store. When we got home my father had calmed down. The judge refused to force my mother to cook, but the damage was done. The ice cream was spilled and, as bound by the era as my father, my mother never talked back again.

Close to the time of her death, my mother told me she had once been offered a scholarship to college. Aghast, she had refused, unable to conceive that she might have intellectual and creative gifts of her own. Woman's place was in the kitchen and there she stayed, after her one brave attempt to defect.

Times have changed, but not as much as it might seem. A friend who is a successful writer showed some of her work to her husband when they were first married. He dismissed it as meaningless drivel. She dutifully forgot about writing and gave her complete attention to the care and feeding of her husband, carrying his image of her as a good wife should. Only after they were divorced did she pick up her writing again and see how good it is. Only then did she take herself seriously enough as a writer to give it the energy and attention that have led to her success.

By the same token, Sallie was once an outstanding weaver. When she married Ralph, a painter, he explained to her that weaving is not art and urged her to take up painting. She complied. She considers Ralph's work to be better than her own, and when he comes to her studio he often picks up a brush and corrects her images. She is grateful for his help, having learned from her father, who is an art expert, to defer to masculine authority in this matter as in others. When she developed cancer Sallie returned to weaving, where her energy flows naturally and lovingly into the work, but self-doubt haunts her still. As a weaver she violates Ralph's image of her and refuses to carry the woman within him on her back. If she does not do it, maybe another woman will. Perhaps the role she has played in relation to Ralph *is* her life, her fulfillment as a woman.

For centuries, women have existed to carry the psyches of men, just as the function of horses has been to carry people on their backs. Until quite recently, men and women alike have accepted that this is the natural order of things, unaware that it prevents them both from becoming whole. Seen in historical perspective, the notion that a woman might be someone in her own right, with a fully separate identity, is revolutionary. The idea that a man has a feminine side that could develop into something different from the woman with whom he lives is equally fantastic.

With rare exceptions, the drive for men and women to become fully functioning human beings, distinct from one another, is brand new. Never having been here before, we have all too few role models or precedents for such a development. No wonder it is so hard! After so many centuries of being horses, no wonder it is so desperately difficult for women to decline to be only what their men imagine them to be. No wonder the inner pressure to become individuals emerges so explosively in women. No wonder it is so hard for all of us, men *and* women, in this time when the creative psyche has begun to make its claim.

In a lecture given in London in the 1930s, for which the manuscript appears to be lost, Jung is said to have predicted a great outpouring of creativity at the turn of the century, as an old eon comes to an end and we move into the new millennium. Now, in the 1980s, a massive wave of creative energy is clearly visible. At the same time we are meeting the archetypal feminine, the resurgent Great Goddess in her many forms. It is no coincidence that creativity and the feminine come forth together. This culture's collective consciousness, composed of the myriad assumptions that dominate our values, perceptions and choices, is fundamentally masculine (patriarchal). The collective *un*conscious of a patriarchal society, the source of its big dreams, carries the values excluded from consciousness and therefore has a feminine (matriarchal) bias. Creative individuals today are compelled to abandon patriarchal ground and descend to the murky realm of the mothers to bring forth what presses to be born into the consciousness of a new age.

To journey into another reality is always perilous. A man may particularly fear the creative process because, in entering matriarchal space, he feels his masculinity to be at risk. Beginning an intense period of painting, Jon dreamed that he was drawn irresistably into the house of an unknown woman, thence directly to the room where she kept her sewing machine. On the machine was a spool of red thread. Jon went straight to it, feeling that he *must* have a piece of the thread, but afraid that the woman who owned the house would catch him there. How would he explain his presence? He pulled out a length of the thread and tried to break it off. The woman came closer and closer. The thread was too strong to break. Jon awoke in fear, looking for something with which to cut the thread, unable to leave it behind but terrified that the woman would catch him.

I have seen the image of the red thread in several artists' dreams, and believe it symbolizes the vital, emotional connection to the feminine without which truly creative work is impossible. This dream reveals a creative man's risk of not being able to "cut the cord," and the danger that he will be trapped in the matriarchal unconscious if he enters it and tries to get a piece of the red thread. Because Jon had a severe psychotic episode several years ago, he is especially sensitive to the possibility that he might not be able to return from the psyche's depths.

The psychology of a creative woman is somewhat different, for the realm of the mothers is her most fundamental reality. To fulfill her creative destiny a woman must become grounded in the divinity in whose image she was made—goddess, not god. When she succeeds, she no longer asks the men in her life to be gods. Then they cease to have the power to subvert her creative life, but are freed to live their own if they can overcome their fear.

Even though her feminine identity is not at risk, a woman makes some of the same sacrifices a man does to be creative. Both must submit to the direction of the collective unconscious, which usually means giving up the wish for power and prestige in a patriarchal culture. Jean, an accomplished writer with an intense need to communicate her inner experiences, consulted me because of a severe writing block. Soon she dreamed:

"My mother has written some poetry. I read it and it is really good. It has my idiom, my style, but is better than I can do. It makes me very jealous and unhappy."

Jean's outer-world mother is not a writer. The dream suggests that her writing block might result from her wish to write from consciousness rather than putting her ability into the service of the images wanting to emerge from the unconscious (her "mother's" writing). After we discussed this possibility the character of her dreams changed completely, emerging as extraordinary examples of the unconscious psyche's "writing ability." The first of many such dreams:

"I was back-packing with a man friend in the High Sierra. We were sitting in a meadow next to a stream. The stream flowed into a small lake, and tall jagged peaks rose above. The meadow was full of flowers, butterflies, birds and small animals. The sunshine had a special, brilliant clarity about it.

"Suddenly a strong wind came up, the sky clouded over, the temperature dropped, and it started to rain. The water felt like it was going through us. We found a cave and crawled in. The roof was too low to sit up, so we lay down and went to sleep.

"Next it was dawn and my friend was gone. I looked out through the narrow cave opening: Instead of the bright meadow, the world outside was barren and desolate. The meadow had shriveled, the stream dried, the lake stagnated. Earth and sky were grey. The sun was rising, brilliant but somehow stark.

"A tarantula crawled onto my knee and sat watching me. I stroked her fur. She went over to the cave opening and started to spin a web across it. I was mesmerized by the spinning. First I thought the web was unusually rich and beautiful. Then, as I looked more closely, I realized that it was a microcosm: There were mountains, trees, rocks, birds, flowers, all making up the filaments. Then I saw that, as the web grew, pieces of the world outside the cave would disappear, reappearing again in the web. The world in the web began to look as the meadow had the day before, sparkling, abounding with life, but in miniature. Then I felt myself being entwined in the web, and I was sitting by the stream in the meadow again."

Thus can the collective unconscious speak under some circumstances, using a person's writing ability to record the inner images and events. It is as if Jean has been "chosen," in the religious sense, to bring forth contents that her mother the goddess wants to make more widely known. What she thinks she wants to write is beside the point.

As we move toward the close of the century, the goddess—the mother world, the creative psyche—exerts enormous pressure, and increasing numbers of people find themselves in Jean's position. Because our culture has buried essential aspects of the human spirit, pushing them to the center of the earth where they have slowly grown to white heat, they now burst forth with volcanic power. The eruption is natural and inevitable, its effects on human life both positive and negative. It brings renewed spirituality and extraordinary creativity hand in hand with psychosis, life-threatening illness, burnout, and the breakdown of social forms.

Many who feel the impact of this influx from the collective unconscious are artists. Others are not, but are distinguished by what I have come to think of as the psychology of the creative person who has an overriding need to give birth to the images and ideas that arise within. Expression is therapeutic for them, and if they do not express they may become ill, physically, emotionally or both. For this kind of person, images unexpressed are poison to the system.

Creative people often find themselves crucified on a conflict between the requirements of everyday outer reality and the inner life that screams to come out, *will* come out in one way or another. Classically this has been the artist's conflict, frequently expressed as a fear that one will prostitute oneself if one creates to sell rather than from the purity of one's inner vision. The same conflict dominates the creative person who is not an artist. It stems from the fact, known deep in the psyche but usually unconscious, that creative vision almost always conflicts with existing cultural values. Creativity brings forth images of new gods that challenge or destroy the old, while established consciousness necessarily holds to the old gods.

A young man's parents once sent him to me with the complaint that he periodically went crazy and tried to smash everything in sight: furniture, windows, dishes, whatever was at hand. Sometimes he even pissed on the floor. He had been given pills to calm him down, large doses of good advice about shaping up and living right, but he still smashed things. Although he had no conscious wish to be destructive, he felt powerless to change the pattern. I discovered that he liked to paint and urged him to do more of it. His untrained work was sensitive and expressive. So long as he kept at it the compulsion to smash things abated, but whenever he stopped painting for any length of time the urge to destroy overtook him. It was as if, when he failed to paint, the goddess possessed him in her black aspect. She *would* be served, and if not through creation then through the destruction that is her other side.

The dark face of the goddess is visible in the psyche at this time in widespread personal upheaval, particularly in loss of orientation between men and women. Her anger reasserts the values of the earth, the primitive and the instinctive. She reacts in anguish against the lopsided development of a technology whose irreverence and disrespect for nature has gone too far. In cancer, almost epidemic just now, she declares herself in a way that cannot be ignored. The uncontrollable assertion of cell growth gone mad gives terrifying concreteness to her insistence that she must have some attention before the values of the feminine are lost forever, and with them the earth.

Some forms of cancer appear to result from an inability to balance an intense creative drive with the requirements of everyday life; that is, from a failure to resolve the creative conflict. This conflict is particularly poignant for women because the personal, particularly in relationship, is central to the spirit of woman. I have never forgotten a cartoon I saw in *The New Yorker* many years ago: One woman talking to another says something like, "I make the little decisions, like where we live and what we eat and where the kids go to school. My husband decides the important things like who should be president and what to do about the war in Vietnam." The truth behind such humor may explain why women's art often wants to be more personal and subjective than is compatible with patriarchal forms.

Three women with whom I work analytically have all dreamed the same archetypal image. All three are gifted artists. One has cancer and one has had several psychotic episodes. All suffer deeply from the creative conflict, an excruciating tension between the demands of financial survival, husband and children, on the one hand, and an intense need to paint, write or sculpt, on the other. All three dreamed that the moon is moving closer to the earth, requiring the dreamer to make a major personal effort to prevent moon and earth from colliding.

The moon symbolizes the feminine archetype, the goddess that exerts a powerful force upon the earth at this time. This dream's recurrence among creative women shows what an extraordinary effort such women must now make to prevent their lives from being destroyed. It is as if the goddess were angry with how we are living, and refuses to go on being cut off from life and overlooked as she has been throughout the Judeo-Christian era. She demonstrates that she has the power to destroy individual lives and even the earth itself. If we fail to pay attention we will be "moonstruck," that is, lunatics.

Lunacy and creativity are two sides of the same coin. Breakdown of body or psyche is the first phase of a creative process which, like the paradoxical genius of nature itself, aims toward wholeness, a moonlike condition in which light and dark are of equal value and import. Whenever an individual or a society becomes too one-sided, too separated from the depth and truth of human experience, something in the psyche rises up and moves to restore authenticity. Breakdown momentarily sets life free from the demands of ordinary reality and activates a profoundly spiritual process, an inner rite of passage with its own healing end. If its creative purpose aborts when we fail to understand the symbolic language it speaks, it is not the process which is at fault.

Whether or not such a process achieves its goal or remains stuck in insanity depends in part upon the individual's willingness and capacity to work with its images and express them creatively. Jung pointed out, for example, that a crucial difference between James Joyce and his schizophrenic daughter Lucia was that Joyce worked on the material of the unconscious and developed it in his writing, while Lucia merely drowned in it.[1]

Because of my parents' example and the requirements of their time, which emphasized material gain at the cost of creative expression, I remained dangerously oblivious to the creative pressures within me until my early twenties. Then, during a period of profound emotional distress, I entered Jungian analysis. As soon as I began to explore my dreams I became overwhelmed by unconscious material. Although I continued to function in a part-time job, I spent long hours lying on the bed in the tiny attic apartment where I lived, swept by images and emotions I did not understand. After a few months, some instinct told me to try to give form to the deluge and I began to paint. I showed this work to no one, not even my analyst, for it did not occur to me that anyone would be interested.

Over a period of sixteen years I filled a large portfolio with paintings. I had no training, nor was I inclined to get any, for I did not think of my work as art. In fact, it most certainly is not if the standards of those who make fashions in art are applied to it. Reflecting upon it now, however, I see that it has the mark of art's origins, wherein men and women found themselves compelled to make images of what moved them and moved within them, driven by an impulse akin to the religious. Is such work, then, religion? Only in the original sense of the word religion, whose probable root meaning, "to bind back," hints at a bond between human beings and something greater, something that is activated whenever self-reflection begins and deep levels of the psyche stir.

Still, my own painting is no more acceptable to the standards of religion as it is practiced in the churches than to the temples of art. There is a third thing that the paintings *are*, neither art nor religion but

---

[1] *C.G. Jung Letters* (Bollingen Series XCV), ed. G. Adler and A. Jaffé (Princeton: Princeton University Press, 1953), vol. 2, p. 266.

related to both: they are healers. They embody an ongoing process of psychological healing and development that is mine, yet does not belong to me. Weighted as it is with archetypal content, such a process reaches into the pain of the very earth and touches the profound wounds that contemporary humankind have in common.

When I completed my training and was certified as a Jungian analyst I stopped painting. I was not aware of a reason for stopping. I just did not feel like doing it any longer. At the time I did not sufficiently understand that I had become a card-carrying member of a patriarchal institution like any other. In becoming an analyst I "joined the group," and immediately fell into contradiction with myself as an artist. Certainly I had no conscious idea that my creative daimon, if permitted to live, would be compelled to move in opposition to the system simply because it *is* creative and the images it generates challenge established gods. I just quietly stopped painting, and quickly forgot its vital connection to the healing process to which I had devoted long hours for many years.

The sense of taboo that affected me then is deeply embedded in the Judeo-Christian tradition. The second of the Ten Commandments clearly prohibits making pictures of what emerges from the depths: "Thou shalt not make unto thee any graven image, or any likeness of any thing that is in heaven above, or that is in the earth beneath, or that is in the water under the earth."[2]

In his novel *My Name Is Asher Lev,*[3] Chaim Potok writes the story of a hasid's son who is destined to become an artist. Beginning in childhood the boy Asher is compelled from within to draw pictures, to create the images whose very existence violate his father's traditional religious sensibilities. His mother supports him in his innermost need, but to his father the boy remains forever incomprehensible and therefore a threat. The book begins:

"My name is Asher Lev, *the* Asher Lev, about whom you have read in newspapers and magazines, about whom you talk so much at

---

[2] Exodus 20:4, King James Version.
[3] New York: Knopf, 1972.

your dinner affairs and cocktail parties, the notorious and legendary Lev of the *Brooklyn Crucifixion.*

"I am an observant Jew. Yes, of course, observant Jews do not paint crucifixions. As a matter of fact, observant Jews do not paint at all—in the way that I am painting. So strong words are being written and spoken about me, myths are being generated: I am a traitor, an apostate, a self-hater, an inflicter of shame upon my family, my friends, my people; also, I am a mocker of ideas sacred to Christians, a blasphemous manipulator of modes and forms revered by Gentiles for two thousand years.

"Well, I am none of those things. And yet, in all honesty, I confess that my accusers are not altogether wrong: I am indeed, in some way, all of those things."

These sentences capture the essential features of the creative conflict. Crucified, caught between the father world and the mother world, Asher has painted his fate. He is hated by those who believe in the dominant conscious values (the fathers) because the images that come to him from the collective unconscious (the mothers) mock the old gods, but he cannot do otherwise because his creative nature compels him to bring images of new gods into the world. He is none of the things of which he is accused, yet on some level he is all of them; that is, he is a personal human being, but also the carrier of an archetypal fate that interferes dramatically with his personal happiness.

One day last year I lingered over lunch in the Trillium Cafe in Seal Harbor, the small town where I live. The atmosphere was extraordinarily animated. Tuning into conversations at the tables around me, I became aware that everyone in the room was talking about dreams. I was thrilled. A selection of my paintings hung on the walls, together with a written description of how they came into being. Entitled *Painting As Healer,* the show was having a strong and unexpected impact.

A few months earlier I had shown my paintings to a patient, hoping to help her open to the creative spirit. I imagined that if she saw

how primitive my work is it might free her to trust her own dimly
formed creative impulses and follow them into life, instead of wor-
rying about whether or not she was making art. As she looked
through my portfolio she became electrified. She said, "Haven't you
ever wanted to show these?" I told her it had not occurred to me. She
begged me to let her put together a show of the work. Although I
agreed, I trembled with a feeling of taboo. I arranged to be out of
town when the show was hung. When I entered the cafe later that
month I sneaked in like a thief, looking furtively about to be sure no
one I knew was there.

Now, seeing what I can only describe as an inductive effect of the
work on others' psyches, I became aware that it made an opening
into another world for people from all walks of life, people who
would not ordinarily be motivated to notice their dreams or to give
conscious attention to the spirit world in any way.

As I sat in the cafe that day I fell deep into déjà vu. A few years
earlier, when I began reading my poetry in public, many people had
seemed puzzled by the work and some had expressed strong feelings
of discomfort with it, just as some did now with my paintings. Simultaneously, then as now, others had reported that their creativity
was remarkably stimulated by mine. Reflecting upon these events, I
understood for the first time that a certain kind of work, resembling
what Jung calls "visionary art," functions in much the same way as
the shaman in tribal societies. That is, some art is shamanic in function. Formed from collective unconscious material, it activates the
unconscious of its audience and mobilizes the psyche's self-healing
capacities. It opens a door to a different reality, the world of dreams
and imagination, and "spirits" silently pass into the world of every
day, affecting people in unexpected ways.

Shamanic art undermines unexamined cultural assumptions. For
this reason it disturbs some people and may even arouse rage. Those
who are open to it, however, often find that it sets their own creativity in motion.

Such art tends to be prophetic. It asks, even insists, on being
heard, just as shamans are compelled to tell about their inner experi-

ences when they begin to apply what they have learned about healing themselves to the healing of others. The visionary creative act is not complete until it finds an audience, coming out into the world and disturbing the complacent surface of collective consciousness. If the process is blocked, one outcome may be psychosis. Cancer may be another.

Shamanic art brings eros values to the healing of the psyche. That is, unlike traditional clinical psychology and psychiatry, it is more concerned with connecting and making whole than with the logos values of dissecting and understanding. It is related to a form of psychotherapy that interprets rarely, seeking instead to set in motion a symbolic process that has its own unforeseeable healing goal. Understanding of behavior is important only to the extent that it serves a living relationship to deep levels of the psyche. Since it is fundamentally creative, this approach to psychotherapy sacrifices the claim to clarity, undermines unexamined assumptions and is more disturbing to than supportive of conformity. The soul of the shaman lies equally behind the visionary artist and the therapist who works in this way. If the shamanic type of therapist ceases to live her own creative life, the capacity to function in healing ways becomes lost and may even turn destructive.

Had I not inherited the problem of unlived creativity from my father, I might have absorbed it from the peculiarly rigid character of contemporary life. A major—perhaps *the* major—psychological task of our time is to rescue the creative life of the spirit from destruction by the ossified patriarchal values and lifeless materialism that characterize a large segment of the world today. I believe that the planet's survival may depend upon the number of people who are able to engage this task.

Speaking as a woman, however, my most compelling reason not to shirk the full burden of my creative life is personal. To the extent that I fail to come to terms with its difficulties, I will simply pass them on, unaltered, to my son Nick—as my father did to me.

Not long after I began to address the problem of creativity in a serious way, Nick dreamed that I had written a letter, as yet unanswered, to a prestigious author. In his dream, Nick and I find ourselves together near the place where the author lives, an apartment that is made to look empty and deserted, its doorway blocked by a huge seashell. With the help of a friend, Nick finds out how to gain entry. The author responds by inviting me to come in. But, in Nick's words:

"My mom is scared to go in, and she sends me in instead. The author sits in a wicker chair. I sit opposite him. The room is dark. He holds mom's letter in his hand and starts to respond as if I had written it. I'm waiting apprehensively for him to ask me a question about it. I'm trying to remember everything he says so I can relay it back to mom. I know there are questions she wants answered, but I don't know what she would ask."

The dream speaks for itself. If I am not to burden Nick with the tasks in life that are mine, I must overcome my fear and discover what the author in me wants to say. Why has he been locked away in a dark and empty place? I must find a way to let him out and ask him my questions directly.

3

Telling the Truth

Her mouth hurt and the alien taste did not go away. The man—her father—was zipping up his fly. Annie began to cry. When he finally spoke, his black eyes burned the words into her four-year-old mind:

Don't you tell. If you tell, I'll kill you.

Annie didn't tell for almost fifty years, but when she began analysis with me, old memories started to come to the surface. Whenever she neared the memory of her father's oral rape of her she panicked. It was so dark a secret she dared not know it herself, lest she die for it. Her husband confirmed her secret conviction that she must be a terrible person to have been treated so badly. She must have brought it on herself. When she told him some things she had read about child abuse he said, "That's awful! If anything like that had happened to *you,* I wouldn't have anything to do with you."

How *could* Annie remember what had happened to her? How could she tell the truth to herself or to anyone?

As I sat facing her, feeling her fear and pain and the unknown secret thing that pressed to be spoken, I realized for the first time that I, too, learned silence young. I must have been three or four years old, because I remember the big pink blossoms on the wallpaper in the dining room where we lived then, and the mahagony refectory table set for lunch. My father told me to wash my hands. I sneaked a glance at them. They looked clean enough, so I said I had already washed them. He told me to wash them again.

Since my father rarely had anything to do with me, his sudden interest in the condition of my hands made me angry. I saw him as a virtual stranger who had no real authority, but I dared not defy him openly. I went into the bathroom, turned on the water for a few seconds without putting my hands in it, and returned to the lunch table.

My father asked, "Did you wash them?" I lied that I had. He pursued the question: "With soap?"

"Yes," I said, determined to bluff it through. He left the table abruptly and I heard him go into the bathroom. When he came back he announced that the soap was dry.

I do not know what happened then. He may have spanked me, but if so I have repressed the memory. What I recall is humiliation so profound I still cringe when I think of it.

Later I started kindergarten. I remember skipping the six blocks home with my first report card, a 9 x 12 piece of paper folded in half. I was eager for my mother to read it, but the news was not good. It reported that I was a tattletale. I had no idea what that meant, but the atmosphere told me it must be very bad. The next day my mother and I had a conference with the teacher, who explained that a tattletale is someone who tells what other people say and do.

This experience, too, was fraught with humiliation. Clearly, the two worst sins were to lie and to speak the truth. Silence seemed my only option.

When I grew up I wanted to be a writer, but the taboo against telling stood in the way. Putting words into the world felt much too dangerous, so I wrote in secret and kept the author in me hidden. Meanwhile I entered a profession whose customs would support silence. As an analyst, I ask my patients to tell the truth, for only then can they learn to know themselves deeply. Professional sanctions require me to protect them from idle gossip by not talking about what they tell, but sometimes more harm results from silence than telling the right person the right thing at the right time. As secret as a priest's confessional, the prescribed analytic atmosphere too often strengthens the guilty sense of sin ghosting about the notion of self-knowledge. When I lose sight of professional secrecy's purpose and take it too rigidly, I feed my patients' neuroses as surely as if I said to them, "It's all very well for you to tell *me* who you are, but God forbid that anyone else should find out!"

Fear of being seen as we are, rather than as we wish to be, is the most common neurotic problem of our time. We are the people who value image more than truth, like Hans Christian Anderson's Emperor who was "so exceedingly fond of new clothes that he spent all his money on being well dressed." Like that very same ruler and all the people in his kingdom but one small child, we are afraid to say what we see lest we be thought "unfit for our office or unusually stupid." Our collective capacity for denial seems to have reached a limit, however, and we now have to deal with a deluge of shocking disclosures: of widespread child abuse, of rampant drug and alcohol abuse, of unethical behavior on the part of prominent citizens—all hidden behind impeccable public images.

Among psychotherapists, some strange customs spring from the split between image and truth. I once sat in a professional meeting whose purpose was to discuss the problems that arise when therapists become sexually involved with their patients. The three men who most loudly opposed the practice were well known for their sexual exploits with patients, but no one mentioned it. *Don't you tell,* whispered the voice of inhibition. *If you tell, I'll kill you.* Like typical children of alcoholics we obeyed, as if we could not see the enormous thing that sat like an elephant in our midst. The taboo against shattering the established image of professional prestige was as effective as the one that forbids a child to say aloud, "Mommy is drunk again," or "Daddy put his pee-pee in my mouth."

Far less impressed by pretension than we, the Kwakiutl Indians of coastal British Columbia brought the need to talk about people into the realm of the sacred, providing ritually for the healthy humanizing function of gossip. When one of my patients dreamed she was given a small box containing a mouth, the image quite mystified me until I saw a carved wooden mouth in an exhibit of Kwakiutl masks. Named Talking Mouth, it represents the right to speak about or criticize other people publicly. At ceremonial events, the person who owns the privilege of Talking Mouth holds it between her teeth, while a speaker standing nearby makes the actual remarks. No one is permitted to take offense at Talking Mouth's comments.

Lacking cultural sanctions for it, how can we learn to speak the truth? How can we reach the inner voices that are drowned by superficial chatter, masked by seductive self-images, inhibited by inner and outer "shoulds" that decry what is real? The way to authentic speech is dark and perilous. For me, it began with a strange dream on my fifty-first birthday:

"I am riding on a train. My traveling companion, a woman somewhat older and more experienced than I, sits in the seat behind me. I have turned to talk with her, speaking over my shoulder. Something, perhaps the expression on her face, causes me to face forward again. I am startled to see myself approaching a small tunnel, barely big enough for my body. It is my own personal tunnel within the train. Others will not enter it.

"Only by lying down abruptly on my back and pressing my arms to my sides do I avoid being dismembered. As I go through the tunnel I am aware of rollers passing over and under me, as if I were a piece of paper on its way through a printing press. I know that when and if I emerge, I will have been shaped to the form of this tunnel and printed with its message. I wonder what becomes of people who arrive blind at this place, not seeing soon enough that survival depends on lying down."

A few days later I could not get out of bed. Whenever I tried to get up, I felt inexplicably exhausted and had to lie down again. The demands of daily life seemed oddly remote. I remembered that "survival depends on lying down" and did not try to force myself to get up, for experience has taught me to pay careful attention when the symbolic patterns in dreams express themselves in ordinary reality. For the next six weeks I spent most of my time in bed, awash with dreams, fantasies and strange thoughts, which I wrote down when I had the strength. Much of the time I slept.

I soon discovered that I could get out of bed for some things and not for others. My psyche appeared to have a mind of its own, quite separate from my conscious wishes, and *it* was in charge. Energy was available to accomplish anything that served its purposes, but whenever I tried to do things unrelated to my inner experience, I immediately felt weak and dizzy and had to lie down again. In time I came to welcome the clues that told me which people and activities were good for me and which I needed to avoid.

My black Labrador dog and three cats moved into the bedroom with me. Every day they arranged themselves in a circle around the bed. When they were not sleeping they stared at me.

A few days before she died, an old woman I knew once told me a cat had come into her house and was sitting there looking at her. She was something of a latter-day shamaness, and felt that the cat was waiting to escort her into the next world. Now I wondered if *I* were dying, perhaps of some rare disease, but I felt peaceful and unafraid, sure that this tunnel in time would deepen my journey through the universe and change me in ways I could not foresee. If the change were death, so be it.

Because I kept my strange symptoms to myself, no one told me I was having a breakdown and I did not think of it that way. Unhampered by a diagnosis, I was free to move through the tunnel and enter shamanic space, the place of the big dream, where I imagined myself to be a snake whose skin would eventually crack down the middle to set a larger me free.

My writing had been blocked for several months. In the past, poetry and prose alike had secretly flowed from my typewriter. Now, caught between two impulses, the uncomplicated clarity of linear thought, and the symbolic, image-laden path of the poem, I could not find my voice in either. I imagined that I would be able to write prose if I could move upward, while poems lay below me, music deeper still. At the very bottom I saw pure rhythm undulating like a vast sea, supporting a moving universe. In my tunnel, however, it was dark and silent and I could not write.

I looked up "tunnel" in the dictionary I kept beside my bed, and wrote down three parts of the definition that touched my imagination:

1. A passage through any extended barrier
2. The main flue of a chimney
3. Middle English *tonel,* a pipelike net for catching birds

Was *I* a bird caught in a net, I wondered?

In a dream two months earlier, my electric typewriter had short-circuited. Before that I dreamed of searching for a new typewriter ribbon because what I wrote with the old one kept erasing itself. Now, in bed, I changed my habit of thirty years and began to use a fountain pen.

One day a poem began to take shape. I wrote:

> every day they gather
> three cats and a dog
> looking at me
>
> they know how to live
>
> cats are cats and
> dogs, dogs
> fat cats fat and
> thin, thin
>
> they don't worry about it
>
> sometimes they want to go out
> or stay home
> sit on a piece of red cotton cloth
> or wool
>   any color
>
> winter has been long and dry
> four pairs of eyes
> watching it

Then I went to the kitchen and made a cup of coffee. When I returned to my bed, the pen had vanished. I could not find it anywhere, then or in the days that followed. I decided to buy a new one, but discovered that Seal Harbor had only ball point pens for sale.

I hate ball point pens. Rather than trying to write with one I bought a deerskin Native American hand drum and taught myself to play it. Day after day its voice spoke from my bed, but my writing voice remained mute. I dreamed:

"Susanna and I are sitting on a bed, singing together."

Long ago, Susanna was one of my first patients. She was a singer then, with a glorious voice. Later she decided to study psychology, and had recently called to ask me to be on the committee to read her doctoral dissertation. So far there was nothing to read. Susanna, too, was having trouble writing.

Musing about the dream, I looked up the word "sing" and found that it stems from an Indo-European root meaning "to make an incantation." Well, I thought before falling asleep again, there is more than one way for a woman to use her voice.

Later I awoke briefly and examined my breasts for lumps. Despite dire pronouncements from the medical profession, I had never done this before and wondered vaguely why I did it now. There were no lumps. The next day my friend Joan called to see how I was. Almost in passing she mentioned that she had found a lump in her breast and had an appointment to have it checked. She sounded unconcerned. I was not unconcerned.

The image of Joan's beautiful face and long red hair was still in my mind when the telephone rang again and shattered it. This time it was Susanna's husband. "Janet," he said, "Susanna has had a stroke. She was terribly upset yesterday because one of her teachers told her she doesn't express her ideas clearly enough. When she woke up this morning she couldn't get out of bed. She can't speak."

I was stunned. Susanna of the beautiful voice, silenced. Susanna who touches the mystery of the psyche, who reaches into poetic depths that *no one* will ever be able to express clearly. My God! Susanna and I, singing from the same bed.

I wrote a letter. It told of my dream and that I, too, was in bed and could not get up. I addressed it to Susanna's husband, and enclosed a note asking him to read it to her even if he thought she could not understand it.

Not many days passed before Colette came to visit. I watched her glasses flash as she talked and rocked back and forth, back and forth in the chair I had put at the foot of my bed. She said I had been in one of her dreams, together with Joan and Joan's husband Richard. I asked her to tell me the dream:

"We women were listening to Richard make a long, intellectual speech ending with the word 'woman!' spoken harshly and with great emphasis. Later I was in Peru, in a town called St. James. I was about to begin a long journey through the jungle to the sea."

I laughed. Long intellectual speeches were arrogant Richard's stock in trade. The part about Peru puzzled me. Colette had never been there and could say nothing about it. So far as she knew, St. James is not a town in the Peru of ordinary reality. I asked her to draw a map of the Peru in her dream, the location of St. James, and the path to the sea. When she finished, the picture looked like a woman's breast. Suddenly she began to sing:

> I went down to the St. James Infirmary;
> To see my baby there,
> Stretched out on a long white table,
> So sweet, so cool, so fair.
>
> Went up to see the doctor,
> "She's very low," he said;
> Went back to see my baby;
> Good God! She's lyin' there dead.

The hair on the back of my neck prickled. I asked Colette if she had spoken with Joan recently. She had not. I could see she knew nothing about the lump in Joan's breast, but something knew. Her psyche was affected and I wondered if she, too, were in danger. My psyche was also affected. Immersed in images of sickness and death, I had a dream that took me back twenty-one years, to a time when I almost died:

"I am setting up a slide projector to look at some newly-processed pictures. I began the roll of film twenty-one years ago, finished it last year, and have only now had it developed."

Exactly twenty-one years before the dream, I was in my seventh month of pregnancy. While trimming the ivy in front of my home I saw a blinding flash of light and got a headache so severe that I had to lie down. When the headache was no better the next day, I went to a doctor. He gave me aspirin and sent me home. I knew that what I had was no ordinary headache, but I could not convince the doctor. He was the authority. Even though it was *my* body, neither he nor I believed I knew what I was talking about. Every day I went to a different doctor. My headache worsened and I began to see double. No one took the symptoms seriously until I went to Dr. Moses, my obstetrician, for my monthly pregnancy checkup. Suddenly he hospitalized me and ordered a series of tests. A spinal tap revealed blood in my spinal fluid, and an arteriogram located the aneurysm that had ruptured in my brain and had been leaking blood for two weeks. I was lucky to be alive.

Dr. Moses was intensely anxious about me. He ordered me to stay flat on my back in the hospital bed and to move as little as possible. Kent, my husband of only two years, was terrified. To quell his fear he adopted a cool demeanor and went to the library to read about cerebral aneurysms. When he came back, he said he was less concerned that I would die than that I might become paralyzed, leaving him with a vegetable on his hands for the rest of his life. As long as my fate remained uncertain, he visited me as little as possible.

Because I was pregnant, the brain surgeon who was called in decided not to operate on the aneurysm. Instead, he clipped a carotid artery. If I were lucky, that would reduce the pressure on my brain long enough for the rupture to heal. The clip was equipped with a tiny silver screw that protruded from my neck. It could be released by anyone at any time if the operation should prove to have been a fatal mistake. Nurses in attendance around the clock carried a small silver screwdriver.

An older woman named Mrs. Green was in the other bed in my room. She also had an aneurysm. Soon after my operation, blood-curdling noises issued from her throat. I imagined that someone in the room was marked for the grave, and decided grimly that I would not go. While she died, slowly and noisily, I gritted my teeth and kept repeating to myself, "It's her or me."

Later her husband sat on her bed crying over and over, "Just a little while ago she was sitting up and brushing her hair, as pretty as you please." I hated them both, and secretly believed that the intensity of my own wish to live had killed Mrs. Green. Sometimes I wonder still.

For several weeks I could not sleep. Whenever I closed my eyes I saw masses of green ivy climbing rapidly down from the ceiling to strangle me.

Every morning a new group of student doctors came by to guess at my diagnosis and try to answer the question of the hour: What anesthetic could be used when I gave birth, to reduce the probability that I would die in labor? Together they arrived at a sophisticated combination of substances that Dr. Moses assured me would keep my blood pressure at a safe level.

Labor began a month later at midnight. After two hours I told the nurse that my baby was on his way out. She laughed and said it was much too soon. Nick was born at three a.m. without benefit of anesthetic. Dr. Moses arrived barely in time to witness the birth. Saying it would be too great a strain to nurse the baby, he gave me some pills to dry up my milk before I had time to think about it. Even in my disappointment it did not occur to me to refuse them.

A few months later I became pregnant again, my first and only unplanned pregnancy. I thought there might be a connection, perhaps a biochemical one, between pregnancy and my ruptured aneurysm.

While most of the effects of the aneurysm had healed, I asked Dr. Moses for an abortion because I was afraid to have another baby so soon. At that time, the only legal basis for abortion was a demonstrable danger to the mother's life. Dr. Moses argued that no link between pregnancy and aneurysms had been proved. However, he agreed to perform an abortion if I would also have a tubal ligation because, he said, I would otherwise just turn around and get pregnant again.

I was only thirty years old and did not know whether I would ever want to have another baby. For two months I agonized, not wanting to make such a final decision. In the end I agreed because I felt I had no choice. It was too soon to risk another pregnancy. My new baby needed a mother more than I needed the possibility of a second child.

I was a good patient then, calm and unemotional in the face of crisis, cheerful and cooperative, perfectly obedient to doctor's orders. But when these events came back to me twenty-one years later, I was flooded with pain, anxiety, grief and rage, tormented by questions long unanswered. When the aneurysm ruptured, why had I not been able to convince a doctor that something was terribly wrong? Why had I hidden my pain at my husband's coldness while I was ill? Why had the nurse ignored me when I said my baby was about to be born? Why had I not insisted on nursing him? Why had I agreed never to have another child? Why had I failed to cry out in horror at the whole experience?

What was the matter with my voice?

I dreamed:

"A tidal wave of cosmic proportions is approaching Seal Harbor. It will wash over the land and destroy everything in its path. Even though it seems futile, those of us who see the wave coming run into a building and lie face down under some furniture. There is a great and terrible silence. I feel that we will all surely die. Then I hear the wave hit. It breaks over the land with enormous force. Miraculously, the building holds and we will survive. Slowly we go out to see the damage."

For several weeks I awoke screaming in the night, swept by emotions that had waited twenty-one years to be heard. What had I done to my body by repressing my reactions for so long? Would the years of silence make me sick?

Joan's doctor feared that the lump she had found was malignant. A biopsy confirmed it. The night before she had her right breast removed, she dreamed she was in Peru, participating in a ritual sacrifice. She did not realize that Peru is the source of the mighty Amazon river, whose name is reputed to come from a nation of legendary female warriors who ritually sacrificed their right breasts in order to shoot their arrows more freely.

Joan was a nice woman. Nice at all costs. After years of deferring to others, she no longer knew her own feelings. She remembered standing behind a door as a child of six, her hand holding the door's hinged edge. She remembered her father trying to close the door from the other side, not seeing that his daughter's fingers were the obstruction against which he pulled. She remembered her stubborn determination not to scream, not to let her father know the pain that was crushing her fingers, a hurt that could only end if she spoke or cried out.

After she married, Joan deferred to her handsome and charismatic husband just as she had to her father. Soon after the wedding, Richard had an affair with another woman. It was the first of many. He told Joan about each in turn. At first her pain was excruciating but she remained silent, biting her tongue to avoid crying out. Later she felt nothing. It was as if she had forgotten how to feel.

When Joan went into surgery, Richard stayed away from the hospital saying he had some important business to attend to at just that moment. It made me angry, but Joan assured me she did not mind. As cheerful and cooperative a patient as I had once been, it did not occur to her to question the doctor's verdict that she had to lose her breast, for his authority in his field was impeccable.

If Joan were to find her voice, she would indeed have to become a warrior. To find mine, so would I.

Richard came to see me one evening while Joan was in the hospital. As we talked, sexual energy filled the room like a fog, so dense I could hardly think. Suddenly Richard shouted, "Stop trying to seduce me!" I was stunned. Stiffly, he put his arm around me. I felt numb, as if I had been hit on the head. I wondered vaguely if I had caused the sexual feelings that had sprung up, and blamed myself for being there alone with him. I knew his reputation for womanizing. Why had I invited him in? I felt confused and guilty. Unable to speak I began to cry, deep wracking sobs.

It was an ancient pain. Falling into a vision, I found myself in a small house in another place and time. I sat in a rocking chair and held my grey cat on my lap, petting her, petting her. It was dusk. A crowd gathered outside. The low, ominous mutter of angry voices grew louder and louder. I knew that they would soon take me out to burn me. Passive in the knowledge that I could not escape my fate, I sat quietly petting my cat in the deepening twilight.

Richard cleared his throat, his eyes on the door. He took a comb from his pocket and groomed his blond hair until every lock was in place. Then he put on his coat and left.

Later that night I awoke in a cloud of self-loathing so profound I wanted to die. I recognized the voice of a killer, a voice that is not my own but finds lodging within me. Fraught with unexamined cultural assumptions, it parrots what "everybody" says and murders individual truth in the womb. It amplifies the words of physicians and other experts, making their power so absolute that it overrides the evidence of our own bodies and souls and causes us to deny our experience rather than question what is handed down from above. This voice, sometimes called the animus, is self-righteous and rigid, bent on suppressing everything natural and spontaneous. It speaks the words and feelings of the angry, witch-burning crowd, wears a patriarchal face and, just because we are women, accuses us of creating the irrationality, the raw emotion, the sexuality, that it fears. It is the voice with which Richard spoke to me, and its echo reverberated far into the night.

Speaking from within and without, the voice threatens on and on: *Don't you tell. Don't you dare say what you really feel and think. Don't give voice to your true experience. If you do, I'll kill you.*

Colette and Henry, her housemate and lover, were having problems. Colette was a budding painter, and whenever Henry was in the house she involuntarily became so absorbed in him that she could not paint, even though he was enthusiastic about her work. She wanted to continue the relationship, but asked Henry to live in a house of his own, separate from her. Hurt and angry, he demanded an explanation. Colette was beside herself. Sobbing, she told me she was dumb in the face of Henry's questions. She did not know how to tell him her feelings. Then, in a dream, she found her voice:

"Henry comes to the house, pulls a gun, and shoots me in the face, right between the eyes. My glasses are broken. I scream, 'I feel so trapped, as if I can't leave the house, and yet I must.'"

Hit in the third eye, the *ajna* chakra of Kundalini yoga, Colette was jolted into the higher consciousness that permitted her true voice to come through. The next day, without stopping to think about it, she expressed herself unambiguously to Henry. Then he could accept what she said. When she realized that she had spoken with clarity she was amazed. She spontaneously hit herself on the forehead with the heel of her hand and exclaimed, "Oh God, I did it!" At that moment, remarkable images appeared in her inner vision. She painted them, all the while complaining to me, "These aren't the kind of pictures I had in mind. I wanted to paint pretty landscapes!" We laughed. Her harsh confrontation with the inner killer had released her real creative voice in spite of the pretty things she imagined she wanted to make instead.

In the meantime I was still flooded with images and emotions as I tried to grasp what was happening to me, to Colette, to Joan and Susanna. Several times I tried to telephone Susanna at the rehabilitation hospital where she was recovering from her stroke. I was worried when I could not reach her, but dreamed that I went to see her and found her speaking quite well, almost completely healed. Then I called and found her at home. She spoke slowly and awkwardly. Some of the words were peculiar, but I understood them when I listened to their deeper meanings, without the ears of conventional linear thought. She said:

"I don't know what to say. It's so complicated. Sometimes there are so many powerful things in saying. It's not important to most of them *why* certain parts of me have been just *trundled,* just *beached!* Someone asked if I knew why I had a stroke and I said my mother . . . reaching fifty . . . my mother deciding not to go on. I got to fifty and then things began to change somehow, just watching for something to happen, not knowing what. And that's it. But sometimes it's utterly different. It's the part about my mother, but it's something else, too. Oh Janet, it's so amazing! It's so hard for it to be so *many* things, but it *is. It's not just one thing.* "

Susanna's mother had died of cancer when she was fifty, and Susanna had always expected to die at the same age. Now she knew she would not, but it had been a close call. I told her I wanted to write a story about her and other women struggling to find their voices, trying to say real things instead of what we imagine our men want us to say. She began to cry. For a long time, only sobs came through the telephone. I waited. When she could speak she said:

"Each time that I cry, I fear that I have lost everything. But it's *not so.* There is something more. We women, what we remember of ourselves is too painful, and something else is wanting to come up."

Yes, I thought, something else certainly *is* wanting to come up. We can't go on any longer doing things the way our mothers did them. If we do, the inner killer will finally get us all.

Spring came early that year. I got out of bed and began to crawl around the house with a flashlight in my hand, looking under all the furniture. Half an hour later I found my fountain pen under the washing machine.

There were strange noises in my house. When I followed my ears, I was led to wild scratchings in the upstairs living room. I opened the door of the woodstove, now unused in the prematurely warm weather, and there was silence. I waited. The scratching began again. Some creature must have found its way into the stovepipe.

Not knowing what to do, I closed the stove door and went shopping. I bought four lined yellow tablets at the office supply store and returned home, where the creature was redoubling its efforts. Helplessly I opened the stove door again. Out shot a strident adolescent starling, screaming its head off. It flew wildly about the room, ramming into windows on every side. I ran after it, along with the dog and cats. The din was incredible.

The bird squawked its way downstairs into the kitchen, flew to the space above a cupboard, disappeared and was silent again. The cats took up a vigil on the floor beneath the cupboard. I waited, but nothing happened.

Late that afternoon, noises issued from my tray cupboard. When I opened it, there was silence. Having dived headfirst among the trays, the bird imagined that if it were very still it would be invisible. I did not ask how it found its way into my cupboard, but reached out and grasped it firmly. Its raucous song resumed. I ran for the front door with dog and cats yipping and yowling close behind, flung the bird out, slammed the door in the face of pursuing animals and watched through the window as this vulgar, admirably vocal, miraculously uninjured bird flew free.

Something jogged my memory. I opened the looseleaf binder in which I had been making notes for the last six weeks. No, I hadn't imagined it. On the first page was a carefully selected portion of the *American Heritage Dictionary*'s definition of "tunnel":

1. A passage through any extended barrier
2. The main flue of a chimney
3. Middle English *tonel,* a pipelike net for catching birds

I thought about it for a long time. Then I picked up my fountain pen and began to write.

4

The Way of the Wilderness

When Joe Rosen walked into my West Los Angeles home-cum-office, I winced and stepped back.

What's *he* doing here? Could this be the person who called for an appointment?

My university training and upper middle-class analytic practice had not prepared me for him. Joe's cocky swagger, black leather jacket and insolent manner ignited my imagination, hinting at a dark world of crime and evil of which I was innocent except in my dreams. An attractive, thirty-nine-year-old divorced woman in the full bloom of my sexuality, I was afraid for myself and for my young son, who was playing quietly in the next room.

Then I saw that Joe was trembling. Poor guy. Scared to death. I relaxed a little and looked more closely. A short man, stocky body, big hands. Veiled brown eyes and full lips in a soft face, a little puffy around the edges suggesting weakness, self-indulgence and vulnerability. Probably a mother's boy behind the bravado. Black hair cut neatly and combed to disguise the balding. He was just short of thirty-three years. We sat down in my consulting room and I tried to bridge the abyss between us.

When I asked why he had come to see me, a secretive little smile crossed his face. I could not read it. He was vague, evasive, said he had had another type of therapy before and felt a need for something to balance it. He had come across some ideas of Jung's, "sensed that a female guide might help him," and that Jungian psychology offered "a way of getting it all together."

I began to see that direct questioning would get me nowhere. He would tell his story in his own time. When I asked if he ever dreamed, he told me the dream he had the night after he called me for his first appointment. I listened with particular interest because the initial dream, so called, may contain both diagnosis and prognosis for analytic work if its message can be understood:

"Me and this woman, we had a motorcycle. We'd be riding through a desert."

A desert? His psychological journey would be on a motorcycle through a desert? My misgivings increased. He added that there was another dream the same night:

"Me and a man and a woman were in a kitchen. The woman was showing the man how to put a slice of ham underneath the salad in a bowl. I said, 'My mother used to do that.' The man was glad for the hint."

I asked Joe to tell me what he could about each image in the two dreams. He did not see the desert as dry and empty at all, but came to life as he spoke of it as a place of mystical transformation. About the ham he said wickedly, "I have a Jewish background, but I like ham." Much later I learned that he had considered going to a Jewish man analyst but had instead chosen me, a nonkosher woman with whom he connected the dream ham. Although the people in both dreams were unknown to him, he imagined that I was the woman.

Man and woman, masculine and feminine, work together in the dream to prepare food in the kitchen, a feminine transformative center. The woman has something to teach the man and he is grateful. She contributes the basis, the grounding, the earth instinct of the pig cooked and ready to be assimilated. Animal life, coming in a form that would have been forbidden to him as a Jew, gives substance to the vegetables on top.

As Joe and I talked, my psyche was responding to the desert dream. The word EXODUS printed itself firmly on the screen in the back of my mind. I ignored it but it did not go away. I told myself, "Don't be silly. Such a grand notion for such a little dream!" It persisted.

I have since learned to pay careful attention to the irrational connections that are generated when I work with unconscious material, but then I was still afraid to trust intrusions into the discussion from "somewhere else." Particularly at this moment, faced with a man whose reactions I could not predict, I wanted to cling to the authority of rational thought. Before the session was over, however, EXODUS had become so distracting that I could ignore it no longer. At last I said apologetically, "You know, I don't know if it makes any sense, but I keep thinking about Moses taking his people out of Egypt into the desert, looking for the Promised Land."

At that moment everything changed. A reluctant look of respect crossed Joe's face, the chip on his shoulder disappeared, and he became a different person. Passionate interest, enthusiasm, warmth and hope filled the room. A spark flew between us and we communicated. He began to reveal his wide knowledge of mythology, religion and alchemy, and an intuitive understanding of the symbolic language of dreams and depth psychology.

We talked about what it might mean to leave Egypt and set out into the desert. He laughed and said, "I work on the pyramids." He was referring to his job in a large department store where he had worked the swing shift for many years, unpacking boxes in a dark basement room, eight hours a night with little break, under constant pressure to work faster. He had begun on the lowest rung of the ladder and never asked for any kind of change, hating every minute of it. I asked why he hadn't moved, if not out of the store, at least to more human work within it. With self-loathing he told me it was comfortable. A steady check, no demands so long as he did the job, no big hassles.

Recently he had come to feel he could not stand it any longer. "It's like a *panic* now. What am I going to *do?"*

Only much later did I begin to understand the full extent of Joe's spiritual bondage. On the one hand he was in subjugation to the Great Mother, the "fleshpots" of body and matter, a matriarchy into which the spiritual masculine cannot enter as an equal partner. On the other, he desperately needed the help of the feminine to ground his spiritual urges. As a result, he was profoundly and explosively ambivalent toward the women in his life as well as the woman within him.

Only later did I see the deeper implications of the desert, where man meets the spirit in the form of gods and demons, and the motorcycle that Joe rode, modern man's power-driven mechanical substitute for the natural carrying power of the horse. I did give some thought then to Moses, who wandered in the wilderness for forty years, repeatedly chastised by God for his arrogance. Moses did not want his calling and did his best to avoid it. Even after he finally led his people successfully through the desert, he was not himself permitted to enter the Promised Land. Wondering how much of his journey the Exodus image foreshadowed, I was prompted to warn the latter-day Moses who sat facing me:

"This isn't an easy route."

He drew himself up, swelling visibly as his cocky smile and insolent manner returned: "I've been through a lot. I can take it."

I shrugged, doubting he knew what he was saying but hoping he did. Optimism seized me and fascination overcame my fear. I had been looking for Joe for a long time, even though I could not have said exactly what I was waiting for until he came. The year before, I had completed my Ph.D., and then been given permission to begin the final portion of my specialty training as a Jungian analyst. I had been looking ever since for what is called a "control patient," and by the end of our first hour I had tagged Joe Rosen "it." For a year or longer I would work intensively with a senior analyst to understand Joe's dreams, fantasies and life history, as well as the ways in which my psyche interacted with his. Then I would write a paper about my work with him and a committee of six analysts would examine me orally upon this work to decide whether I was qualified to be an analyst.

Nowadays trainees are encouraged to select control patients whose analyses will predictably show to good advantage before the examining committee, but in my time more room was left for students to make and learn from their own mistakes. Since I believe that the success of analytic work can rarely be judged from the limited perspective of the analyst's office, I was not interested in a "good" control patient. Instead, I waited for someone to make the hair on the back of my neck stand up, having found in that sensation a reliable sign that someone or something is beyond me, yet not so far beyond that I am untouched. It signals the presence of the gods and connects me with my growing edge, where what happens is vital, exciting, difficult and an important source of learning.

Something in me knew during our first meeting that Joe would challenge me to my limits, rub salt in my wounds, and involve me to my most unconscious depths. Something knew that I, who was then most at home in the patriarchal world of reason and performed best in an atmosphere of impersonal truth and objective understanding, would have to rely upon the strength of my feeling for Joe and learn to function therapeutically in the presence of passion and violence. Something knew that tolerance for paradox and doubt needed to replace my wish for certainty, that this person would require of me the most rigorous honesty, and that he would finally leave me with a sense of inferiority and failure. In short, I guessed that Joe Rosen would be the ideal whetstone to hone the tools of my healing trade, without any real idea of what I was in for.

Pieces of Joe's story emerged over many months. He was born in in Chicago of atheistic Jewish parents. With boundless contempt he portrayed his father Max Rosen as rigid, power-driven, materialistic and concerned only with what the neighbors might think. His mother, six years dead, was an ambivalent figure. Sometimes he hated her, usually not. "She had something," he said. "She had a lot of potential that never came to fruition." Sophie Lap was born of Baltic peasant stock and came to the United States as an adolescent, unable to speak a word of English. Joe described her as an intelligent but uneducated farm girl who lacked social grace and whose earthy, primitive ways repeatedly frustrated Max's social ambition.

Joe's sister Maxine was born when he was seven. He had little to say about her except that she was "okay," still less about Sam, the brother who arrived a year after Maxine. For years before our work began he had had no contact with his family, refusing even to attend his mother's funeral. Max had remarried. "I guess he works in Hollywood. He lives someplace in Santa Monica. I can't be around my relatives without getting all fucked up. It brings me down, tears me up. They're typical Jewish-type people."

Joe's antisemitism was passionate and extreme. "The Nazis had a good point," he said. "It's too bad their plan didn't succeed!" When I pointed out that he was Jewish he was enraged and insisted that he most certainly was not. His parents were Jewish, but he was not and neither was Ruth, his (Jewish) girlfriend. I was bewildered until I realized that in his vocabulary "Jewish" meant pushy, overbearing, materialistic and overly ambitious, roughly equivalent to what I would call the Jewish shadow.

Before Joe reached school age his family moved to Los Angeles. Here he first became aware of his heritage, when neighborhood children stood outside his house shouting "Dirty Jew!" This is one of his earliest memories.

Seen symbolically, as if they were dreams, an adult's earliest memories can reveal structural aspects of the psyche that will dominate most or all of his life. The images are like snapshots of the psyche's deepest layers. Joe's memory of being called "Dirty Jew," not knowing what it meant but feeling that it must be very bad, is a picture of his lifelong tendency to become identified with evil, a tendency that is common among people raised in abusive or neglectful environments. The other side of the picture was his wish to separate himself entirely from this painful image by claiming not to be Jewish at all. He thus alternated between the two poles of his early memory, becoming in turn the tormenter and the tormented, Nazi and Jew, scapegoater and scapegoat, abuser and victim.

When he was five Joe began to take violin lessons and was, he told me, "damned good." The lessons continued for two years, but Max was determined to make a prodigy of him and "that snuffed out my desire to continue." At about this time Joe developed a recurrent paralysis of the legs, for which no physical basis could be found.

Joe wept when he told me that knowledge and intellectual achievement were the real sin in his parents' house. Books were both fascinating and taboo to him. His spontaneous intellectual curiosity as a child had been the particular object of his father's ridicule. Nevertheless, he did well in school until the eighth grade, when the family moved again and he was put back half a year to accommodate the new school's regulations. Joe was outraged. His parents were not interested in his pain. He felt frustrated, furious and impotent. At that moment, he told me, he threw up his hands and said fuck it all. Thereafter he ignored school and dropped out as soon as he could, although he completed a high-school degree much later.

Not long after he cut himself off from his love of learning, Joe fell in love with a girl for the first time. He worshiped her from afar, never spoke to her, carefully protecting his feelings by telling no one. He did not dare to try to develop a real relationship with a girl until he was twenty-two. Having gradually overcome fears of impotence, he had had a series of girlfriends by the time I met him.

During the time we worked together Joe was with Ruth, a divorced woman several years older than he with a ten-year-old daughter and an adolescent son. The mother-son component of their tempestuous relationship created major difficulties and expressed itself graphically in Joe's dreams. For example:

"I was in the house when Ruth's son came in. I was trying to make him behave. Then she got on me for bothering her kid. Then I got pissed at her and started pushing her around. I ripped a mask off her face. The image of the mask was my mother's face."

Joe began studying karate when he was twenty, and it soon became an important part of his life. His conscious intent was to strengthen his masculine identity. However, in his dreams the forms of karate became connected to the woman within him, the soul image that Jung has named "anima." In Joe's dreams the anima often appeared as a beautiful and graceful young dancer, the object of his love and admiration, skillfully executing ritualistic Kempo movements. In other dreams, when danger approached and threatened to overwhelm him, Joe would protect himself with appropriate ritual movements. For example, he responded to something unknown approaching in the dark with a movement called "Darkness," defending himself from the threat by taking on some of the dangerous thing itself in much the same way that a vaccine protects against disease.

We had worked for more than a year before Joe told me I was his tenth therapist. He had begun to look for a "master" thirteen years earlier, moving rapidly from one therapist to another. Even allowing for exaggeration he must, as he said, have tried just about everything. He refused to discuss any but the most recent therapist, with whom he had stayed for five years. When he went to Dr. Kraft he felt that he had finally met his match. At that time Joe was, he said, "a total innocent." Dr. Kraft indoctrinated him into a megalomaniacal philosophy that identified body with ego and ego with the gods. According to the doctor, only the material world is real, psyche and spirit being side effects of the failure to take control of the body. Control the body and you control the world.

With his immature ego and consequent sense of powerlessness, Joe readily identified with the doctor's vision of physical man as Superman, beyond good and evil, able and willing to do anything for absolute power. He gradually became a privileged member of the doctor's inner circle, learning that the unforgivable sin is attachment, and separation from loved objects is essential. If the will is too weak to effect separation, said Dr. Kraft, it may become necessary to murder the loved one.

When Joe came to me he was still seeing Dr. Kraft. The first visit to me was an attempt, behind both the doctor's back and his own, to move out of bondage to Dr. Kraft's philosophy. This was another dimension of Joe's Exodus.

Innocently I urged him to confront his relationship with the doctor openly and to discuss his misgivings with him. Joe informed me I was most naive. Dr. Kraft was master and was not to be questioned. If even half of what Joe told me about the doctor was literally true, then confrontation would indeed be useless, even dangerous. I could never be sure how much Joe's perception expressed Dr. Kraft's outer reality, and how much it really mirrored the Nazi in Joe's unconscious. In any case he stopped seeing the doctor eventually, but not until we had worked together for many months.

Early in our work and the night after a visit to Dr. Kraft, Joe dreamed:

"I was riding along on a bicycle and was stopped by a big black man, over three hundred pounds. He was putting out cigar butts on my shirt sleeve. I was meekly letting him do what he wanted. I knew that later I'd be alone with him, and could kill him with the karate. I was waiting for my moment. I knew that I was the most submissive victim he had, and because of that the most deadly."

This dream shows the primitive power of the overblown, compensatory masculine image that Dr. Kraft supported, and with which Joe identified in the absence of validation for his individual masculine identity. The fear I felt when we first met was my instinctive response to the weight of the sadist in the unconscious. Joe thought he could put this image on and take if off at will, but the dream shows the extent to which his boyish ego had fallen under its power, becoming a reluctant but necessarily submissive victim of this potent archetype. He would have to develop some real strength if he were ever to break its domination.

As we worked, many aspects of Joe's behavior confused and frightened me. I urged him to give expressive form to some of the images in his dreams. He did, with loving care, showing a fine untrained talent in his delicate watercolors, clay pieces, wood blocks and even stained glass. In sporadic fits of anger and violence he destroyed them all. I encouraged him to follow his intellectual curiosity, and occasionally loaned him books. He read avidly, with great excitement, yet more than once I got up in the morning to find the torn fragments of books I had loaned him scattered on my front lawn. Like some archaic god, he created and destroyed in equal measure. I feared he would go mad if he could not find a way to accept and integrate his intellectual and creative gifts, nurturing them as enduring parts of himself.

From what he told me of his childhood, together with what his dreams revealed of his psychological structure, I surmise that Joe had been a very bright child, probably with an introverted, intuitive nature more like his mother's than his father's. Since Max was the more powerful parent, however, Joe began at an early age to identify with his psychologically abusive father and turn against himself. Some aspects of his natural identity were stuck between the ages of five and seven, when he was assaulted by antisemitism and by the power distortion Max imposed on Joe's relation to music. Something else became trapped at puberty, when he felt compelled to abandon both his interest in learning and his love. He simply ceased to develop.

Over the years Joe protected his undeveloped ego well and it remained healthy but childish, an uninitiated mother's son who craved protection and could not meet a women as an equal. The most serious obstacle to his growth now lay in the three-hundred-pound man, the sadistic archetypal image that often appears in the unconscious following childhood abuse. If he were to dare to be himself, with his childlike spontaneity, warmth and vulnerability, as well as the infantilism and dependence he periodically revealed, he risked becoming possessed by the Superman whose victim he was.

For the first few months Joe and I focused on his outer-world problems and the negative masculine images that peopled his dreams. Many of the men in his dreams embodied a potential for violence and destruction. Some of them, known technically as shadow figures, were ordinary human beings whom Joe disliked but whose characteristics belonged to him and had been suppressed and denied in the course of his development. If he could reclaim the undesirable parts of himself that he had disowned, they would give him strength and substance, a capacity to accept and deal with ordinary reality lacking in people who want to look perfect and cast no shadow.

Other characters in Joe's dreams, like the three-hundred-pound sadist, were bigger than life. Such figures are images of divine or demonic possibilities in the human psyche, mythic factors that anyone who looks deep enough can find inside. These archetypal forces could possess Joe and cause him to become violent if they were released suddenly. Brought to consciousness gradually, however, allowing him to give due respect and consideration to the energy behind them, they would constitute the very foundation of his masculine development.

Myths, fairy tales and even films and novels that catch the spirit of a time or a group of people bear the same relation to the collective psyche that a personal dream does to an individual. Joe had in common with most contemporary American men a piece of inner drama resembling the mental hospital in Ken Kesey's novel *One Flew Over the Cuckoo's Nest*,[1] where the masculine spirit has fallen so completely under the power of the negative mother that healthy male energy is considered sick and dangerous.

In the novel, Big Nurse Ratched rules her mental ward with an iron hand to be sure no dangerous male energy erupts. She has, and does not hesitate to use, the authority to destroy the men's impulses to be themselves by ordering electroshock "therapy" whenever the incipient spirit of manhood rears its ugly head. Protagonist McMurphy, the (at first) irrepressible image of healthy adult masculinity, decides to fight Big Nurse, thinking to bring some measure of spiritual freedom to the men who have fallen under her power. In the end, however, she plays her trump card and has McMurphy lobotomized. A ray of hope remains. Chief Broom, the halfbreed Indian from whose point of view the story is told, refuses to accept McMurphy's lobotomized body. A huge man who has pretended to be deaf and dumb, Broom's instinctive rage is aroused. He finds his voice, compassionately kills McMurphy's soulless body, throws some hospital equipment through a window and escapes.

Kesey's work lays bare some hard truths. When a man lacks powerful and positive male models he feels illegitimate, without a conscious sense of identity and strength. As a consequence he may be overwhelmed by the femininity that lies in his unconscious, becoming possessed by passivity and the expectation that someone will take care of him. The archetypal image of the nurturant female (mother or nurse, for example) then turns negative and the man falls into a chronic state of passive rage against women. For the most part

---

[1] New York: Viking, 1964.

it remains hidden because he is afraid of women's retaliation, but it seeps through in passive-aggressive and covertly sadistic acts. A man who is possessed by "Big Nurse" cannot meet a woman's real strength because he projects the overwhelming bitch-woman upon her. She may, in turn, fall under the archetype's negative power and act out the bitch-woman in spades.

The novel's resolution suggests that Big Nurse's hold might be broken and maleness set free if the primitive psyche were to find its voice. The Chief's spirit breaks through in wildness that is only apparently destructive. His anger is clean and bears a highly differentiated ethical compassion that is only available to real strength.

It is hard for a woman not to be afraid of a man's primitive side. If he is to relate to women, his maleness usually has to be gentled a little, but in its own time. When it is cut off entirely or prematurely, he becomes a manikin who embodies women's unconscious male images rather than real masculinity. On the surface, such a man may appear to be the very model of success, what every mother thinks she wants her son to be. But beneath the surface he is lifeless, disconnected from his feelings and instincts, as devoid of spirit as if lobotomized.

When I began to work with Joe, I did not yet understand that I was drawn to him precisely because he was closer to his primitive impulses than many of the men I knew. I could not help being afraid of the suppressed violence that lurked in the background, but I sensed that he needed to accept and integrate his hidden savagery. I had no idea how, or even whether, he could do it, least of all whether I could bear the process.

Slowly I tried to help him differentiate the outside world from his own psyche in the world, to accept as his own some of the inadequacies he saw in others. He was seized by rage against the intractable people in his life who refused to conform to his idea of who they were. He was afraid that he might kill someone in his anger, and so was I. We worked on ritualistic ways to contain it, using as models the karate movements that protected him from his dream aggressors. Soon he dreamed:

"I met a girl. There were many around her, concerned and caring for her. I found out she was a famous dancer. She had red hair and freckles. She was firm and sturdy, a healthy outdoors type. I wanted to ask her how old she was in order to have a chance to talk to her.

"The dancer had a powerful older instructress. She was really something: very strict, but really a guide. I wanted to tell her that the dancer needed me to make her a better dancer. I'd be good for her sexually. I could see that she was truly a great artist. She had charisma, magnetism, and was really in touch with life.

"Jake was there. In the dream he was an opera singer. I got down on my knees to keep him from flipping out, trying to appease him."

I was happy to see such a healthy, earthy embodiment of Joe's inner woman, well cared for and protected. As she was apparently still immature and unready to be on her own, he could only communicate with her through her teacher. That is, he had not yet acquired the masculine strength to meet the feminine on an equal basis. Nevertheless, the girl had aroused Joe's sexuality and he wanted to try to relate to her.

First, however, he would have to deal with Jake, a fellow department-store employee whom Joe described as a woman-hater and a Nazi at heart. As an opera singer, this shadow figure had a strong voice in Joe's psyche and the power to interfere dramatically with his incipient erotic relationship with the inner woman, a relationship mediated by his work with me. If the Jake within him were not to shatter our fragile connection, Joe would have to get down on his knees and humbly acknowledge his Nazi-like capacity to destroy everything weak, imperfect and therefore human in himself and others.

5

The Two-Headed Serpent

Six weeks after I began working with Joe I had a frightening dream:

"It's time for Joe Rosen's appointment and I go into the waiting room to let him in. He appears not to be there. I call his name and hear a rustling sound in the corner. Suddenly a snake is moving directly and swiftly toward me. I think it is a rattlesnake, although it does not look like one; it is cylindrical, not flat, and has a rich brown tail shading into green at the head. On its head is a green diamond. It is in cobra position, moving directly toward me ready to strike. I feel trapped. I keep thinking, 'If you see a rattlesnake, run like hell,' but if I turn my back on it to run, it could bite me from behind."

I awoke, tense and anxious. Joe had an appointment with me later that day, and I felt I had to understand the dream before I saw him. There was no immediate opportunity to discuss it with my control analyst, so I decided to see what I could learn using a technique called active imagination.

Active imagination is a way of relating to parts of the psyche that are not directly accessible to consciousness. One method is to visualize being with someone, perhaps a dream figure, and carrying on a conversation in writing. It is often hard to accept the validity of what happens during such a dialogue, but if the work is done correctly it gives access to deeper levels of the psyche's wisdom than are usually available. It must be a dialogue, not a monologue, because only conscious participation and confrontation of what comes up can avert the pitfalls of a process like "channeling," wherein the person goes into a trance and any voice that speaks is accepted uncritically.[1]

---

[1] For a more complete description of the work of active imagination see my chapter "Active Imagination in Practice," in Murray Stein, ed., *Jungian Analysis* (La Salle, IL: Open Court, 1982), pp. 173-191.

At that moment I needed help with a problem in Jungian analysis so I decided, in a manner of speaking, to go straight to the top and engage the supervisory services of an inner figure named Jung. I had read almost everything Jung wrote, and therefore had within me a feeling for his way of seeing things that I now hoped to tap to help me understand this particular dream in its precise context. I could have looked up the thousand or more references to "serpent" and "snake" in Jung's *Collected Works,* but there was not enough time, and no assurance in any case that what I found would be directly applicable to my dream.

Having talked with "Jung" a number of times before, I was familiar with the imaginal setting where I could find him. Now I "went there," by visualizing myself approaching his office on the second floor of an old European building that faced a cobblestone town square. When I knocked he opened the door, greeted me warmly and asked what he could do for me. I told him the dream.

Jung said instantly, "You are afraid of the sexual feelings between you and Joe."

I was startled, but upon reflection realized he was right. I did not want to admit, even to myself, how sexually aroused I had become when Joe and I discussed the dream of the dancer. When I protested that I did not know what to do with those feelings Jung replied, "Stay with them, damn it! Carry them. Don't just scream and run."

I said I was afraid of being overwhelmed. "Joe acts everything out. He thinks sex, along with everything else, is something to *do.* He doesn't understand the point of living with sexual energy and letting it fuel a transformation process. The trouble is, sometimes I have my own doubts about it."

Jung replied, "You'd just better get your doubts out of the way. The work with him will stand or fall exactly there. Joe is stuck in the body, the 'fleshpots' of Egypt. He needs you to help him contain the sexual energy. Deal with your doubt and don't let it hang out or you'll both be devoured."

As we talked, I felt more and more insecure about my competence, about the efficacy of depth analysis, about the possibility for psychological change at all. Finally I said, "Maybe I'm not ready to handle such a difficult case. Maybe I should send him to someone who has had more experience."

Jung was furious. To do that would really let Joe down, he said. Joe needed me to stand firm and not permit him to push me out of shape. "Stay real," said Jung. "Stay who you are and be there for him."

Later that day Joe arrived for his appointment. He had had a dream the night before:

"I'm in a kitchen. A green, two-headed snake is moving toward me in a cobra-type position. The heads are strong and firm, with bright, piercing dark eyes. I'm thinking that snakes attack by the brightness of your eyes, and am squinting to cut down the brightness. I'm also trying to keep a distance from it and thinking that snakes only attack when attacked."

I gasped. The extraordinary similarity in the content of our two dreams on the same night could hardly be accidental. We were both about to be bitten. Joe's dream told me that he, too, wanted to ward off the snake by remaining unconscious, cutting down the brightness of his eyes and keeping distance. He did indeed need me to stand firm. His fear was enough for both of us.

Because he was my control patient, I knew it was inevitable that Joe and I would form a special bond. After all, my fate depended upon what happened to him during the year or more of our control work. Still, the power of the love-hate relationship that grew between us stunned me. Only now, fifteen years later, do I begin to understand some of its dimensions.

In analytic work that goes deeply into unconscious material, archetypal/spiritual levels of the psyche are commonly activated. Godlike and demonic projections fall like rain upon the therapist and sometimes also the patient. It is just then, when the analyst has been elevated to divine status, that overwhelming sexual energy is likely to stir. I believe it may express a compensating need for the relationship to come down to earth. It is as if healing cannot take place when the analyst takes or is given too much of the psyche's power. The psyche manifests sexually to humanize and equalize the relationship, making it clear that the analyst is a vulnerable human being like any other.

Acknowledging the patient's importance with an expression of simple human feeling usually reduces the sexual charge to bearable proportions. If the participants are able to carry the residual tension humbly, without acting upon it, the sexual fire will fuel a process that transforms both. If a sexual relationship is lived out, however, I have not yet seen an exception to the rule that the patient is harmed and the healing process subverted. The fact that sex between therapists and their patients has become quite common today shows how far the temptation for therapists to play God has separated the profession from ordinary human feeling and good sense.

Joe and I secretly agreed that what we were doing was very special. It was as if the psyche retorted, "Humph! You may imagine you're *something,* but you are nothing more than two naked human beings struggling with the human condition." Faced with the sexuality that threatened to overcome us, Joe's Superman paled and so did my pretensions to analytic authority. *It* had the power, not we, and it would glue us together during the months that followed whether we liked it or not.

Joe told me about a Kung Fu movement called "the two-headed serpent." In its execution the two hands hit simultaneously, one to the head, the other to the solar plexus, in order to break a stranglehold. "A very ancient movement," he said. He also mentioned the caduceus, a staff entwined with two serpents that is currently used as a sign of the medical profession.

In the ancient world, the caduceus symbolized the power of the god Hermes/Mercury. The alchemists, who "saw" the transformations that occur deep in the psyche projected into chemical reactions, imagined the mysterious and ambivalent figure of Mercury to be a primary catalyst for the healing process. One of Mercury's forms was the snake, whose ability to shed its skin aptly symbolizes the psyche's capacity for radical transformation. Alchemical imagery hints at the god's healing qualities when it describes him as "a peacemaker, the mediator between the warring elements and producer of unity."[2] One alchemical text expresses his paradoxical nature (two-headedness):

"By the philosophers I am named Mercurius; my spouse is the [philosophic] gold; I am the old dragon found everywhere on the globe of the earth, father and mother, young and old, very strong and very weak, death and resurrection, visible and invisible, hard and soft; I descend into the earth and ascend to the heavens, I am the highest and the lowest, the lightest and the heaviest; . . . I am dark and light; I come forth from heaven and earth; I am known and yet do not exist at all; by virtue of the sun's rays all colors shine in me, and all metals. I am the carbuncle of the sun, the most noble purified earth, through which you may change copper, iron, tin, and lead into gold."[3]

I hoped that if Joe and I could permit ourselves to be bitten, to bear the tension of the opposites that lie behind sexuality, the wisdom of love might be born and the Superman's stranglehold broken. I wrote in my journal:

> yesterday
> black and white met
>
> will you come with me
> this thing in-between us
> exploding with hate/love?
>
> black and white
> will meet again tomorrow
> if we are together
>
> do you know that?
>
> or do you lull yourself
> as i do
> hoping

[2] C.G. Jung, *Mysterium Coniunctionis*, CW 14, par. 10.
[3] Quoted in C.G. Jung, *Alchemical Studies*, CW 13, par. 267.

someday
for peace together?

in us
between us
black and white meet

are you ready for it?

Joe was not. The next week he told me this dream:

"The Nazis came. They were rounding up people. I had some money in my back pocket and had to keep it from them. They said we had to be searched. We'd be stripped. There was no way to keep the money from them.

"There were two Nazis. They were very polite. As we were going around a curve I saw a chance to bury my valuables in the sand next to a chain link fence, on my left. Along with the money I buried some blue-chip stamps and some little potassium pills."

In a culture where everything is measured by its exchange value in the marketplace, it is tempting to use love to inflate one's sense of power and self-importance. When that happens, the treasure of love is distorted and its incomparable value subtly diminished. Joe connected the burial of his dream wealth with his childhood habit of hiding things from his parents to protect them from just such misuse. He had kept his love of learning and his sexual interests concealed for this reason, and had stopped playing the violin to prevent his musical gift from serving his father's wish for status and power. Now Joe was afraid his feelings for me would be misappropriated. He buried them rather than risking the possibility that they would fall into Nazi hands as his talents had fallen into Max's.

I did not know whether Joe was afraid of the Nazi in me, in him or both. He certainly had experienced how easily power in the hands of doctor or therapist can turn its shadow face, making a healer into a Hitler. If I wanted to change Joe, to make him into my own idea of what he should be instead of helping him find his own path, the un-expected emotional intensity between us would leave him as vulnerable to my power as he was to Dr. Kraft's. If I were to use him for my own purposes and he did not bury his treasure, he would become my victim.

When I asked for his associations to blue chip stamps Joe said, "I don't use them. I have them lying around all over the place. They're valuable but are too much trouble to use."

I heard in his words an echo of something the alchemists said about their treasure, the philosopher's stone: "It is found thrown out into the street, it is the commonest thing to be picked up anywhere,"[4] and the old song "The Best Things in Life Are Free." In the spiritual world the most valuable things are rarely found in high places but, as Joe said, it is hard work to redeem their value.

What about the little potassium pills? Joe said, "I have too much sodium in my system and have to take potassium. Sodium is for the outside of the cell, potassium for the inside."

The Chinese say that sodium is yang (masculine) and potassium is yin (feminine). It looks as though Joe has an overdose of outer masculine image and, for his health and balance, needs to take something to nurture the inner feminine. However, in the grip of the Superman and following the model of his childhood, he buries the medicine along with the rest of his wealth to keep it from being destroyed.

The dream's meaning was visible in our sessions. Joe's defiant, chip-on-the-shoulder manner returned, replacing the related and vulnerable human being I had come to know and like. For all practical purposes he buried his feelings and became the Nazi. He picked and sniped at me and challenged my competence, testing me at every turn. I knew that I could only lose if I were to tangle with what possessed him. I tried not to fight back, but it was hard. He dreamed:

"I was in a room like my room where we lived when I was eleven to thirteen years old. There was a place in the wall that had been repaired before. I had rubbed on it a lot and it had gotten worn down. It had been very badly repaired. Now I was rubbing on it and a layer broke through and the inside was exposed. Sand began coming out,

---

[4] Quoted in C.G. Jung, *Psychology and Alchemy*, CW 12, par. 103.

and then insects, flying insects like dragonflies. Then it was a nightmare—dragonflies all over. The air was just full of them. I wasn't enveloped by them, but the girl who was there was. I told people to spray inside the wall and close the doors and windows. I was okay—I was near an open window."

The years from eleven to thirteen bracketed the last stage of Joe's childhood self-abandonment, when he hid his interest in school and also his love. He attributed the badly repaired wall to his previous therapies and blamed me for the breakthrough.

Like a tongue that compulsively worries the cavity in a tooth, or an infant's rhythmic rocking, rubbing the wall is a piece of instinctive, ritualistic behavior. Joe's impulse to keep rubbing the same place calls attention to a "hot spot." He knows where his treasure is buried and cannot stay away from it. With rhythmic motions akin to the sexual, he breaks through to his walled-up nature and is invaded by lovely fantasy dragons.

His fear of the insects might be justified. They could signal a latent psychosis, ready to overtake him unless he destroys the alluring images that engulf him. However, he told me he had spent many happy childhood hours chasing dragonflies, catching them, looking at them and setting them free, and I hoped he could follow his fantasies in the same way. Then his spirit might live and grow again. Instead, like a young Nazi, he kills them using the impersonal, indiscriminate techniques modern technology has developed to subdue the myriad forms of nature.

I braced myself and waited to see what would happen. Before many days had passed, a one-sentence note arrived in the mail: "I'm terminating my analysis. [signed] Joe."

Grieved and angry, I felt like a precipitously jilted lover. Besides, I thought guiltily, if he quit now the control work might be judged inadequate. Today I wonder if my wish to use his "case" to gain analyst status was another manifestation of the Nazi archetype that possessed him.

I wrote Joe that analyses are not terminated by mail. Calling upon my superior authority, I told him we would discuss the matter at our next hour. I knew it was hard for him to face the dragonflies, I said, but I hoped he would have the courage to do so. To my surprise he appeared at the appointed time. He was furious. He informed me that I had put him in the untenable position of knowing things that made it impossible to live unconsciously any longer. He shook his fist at me and shouted, "Once you know something you can't not know it. Now I can't go back!"

His anger bewildered me. From my point of view, he was berating me for doing good work. As we talked he grew calmer and explained the problem he was facing. Through Dr. Kraft he had developed an adaptation that worked as long as nothing changed. His Nazi image made his fellow workers leave him alone, and he could overlook the deadening nature of his life so long as he suppressed his fantasies. Now, as he broke through the wall, he felt himself "regressing to an earlier time, when I was in touch with other things."

The other things were values of spirit and soul: love, curiosity, the creative impulse. "But," he said, "when I go to the department store with *that,* they tear me apart. They smell it. I have to be schizophrenic and wear one face here, another there. I can't go on like this."

"If you should drop dead," he said ominously, "I could go back to being stable like I used to be."

Remembering that murder was Dr. Kraft's "cure" for attachment, I shivered. Would Joe try to kill me? I wished I had not insisted he come back for this session, and was not altogether pleased when he decided, for the time being, to continue the analysis. A few days later he had a dream that showed his options:

"I was irritated with my mother because she was being so *nice* to me and I wanted nothing to do with her. There was a large bottle of aspirin that I'd lost somewhere. Where had I left it? I went home and thought I'd found it, but it wasn't the same bottle, it was a different bottle and it really affected me. Inside was water condensation, foliage growing in rich black earth, and a little snake. The snake had the same kind of head as the double serpent. The bottle had a little flowerpot for a cap."

Joe said emphatically, "I *never* take aspirin. It makes holes in your stomach. It's incompatible with my body!"

He wants to leave the matriarchy, to stop being his mother's son, and looks for aspirin to kill the pain. Once consciousness has crept in, however, he can no longer find the easy way out, the mass-produced panacea that is incompatible with his individual nature. What he finds instead, at home in his own space, is a natural and primitive process of development, a veritable Garden of Eden complete with the pain and conflict that inevitably enter with the serpent. He must take up the task of his own psyche.

Joe's dreams began to concern themselves with masculine initiation. First he dreamed of learning to use a knife. Then:

"A voice said to me, 'The word is a star. Star means one.'"

A disembodied voice in a dream often carries the authority of divine revelation. This voice speaks of "the word," probably referring to the divine logos, the masculine God in whose image the Judeo-Christian tradition says a man is made. The star hints at Joe's individual fate, its "oneness" implying the wholeness with which he was born, the unity so badly shattered during his childhood. The imprint of his original unity beckons, reminding him of the dignity intrinsic to his status as a man and a human being.

A few days later he had a long and complex initiation dream:

"I was walking down a dark alley. There was a guy to the left of me and one behind me. I told the one behind me not to follow too close. I needed my complete wits about me to avoid being hit by things in the dark, and he distracted me. I turned around and looked at him. He had a long stick. I jumped and kicked him with both feet, then put the stick through his throat and turned and went on.

"The other guy and I walked into a house. There was a meeting going on like a black mass. The major part of it was a briss [ritual circumcision]. The first person I saw was a woman who was overseeing the whole thing.

"There was a large table with a small white tablecloth. All the Jewish things used in the ceremony were on the table. The ritual going on was to have their kids serve Satan, to make it part of the *whole*. They were specifically reaffirming that if they did this, their kids would be successful in business.

"Set off on another linen cloth were two pitchers of water. They were what, added to the briss, made it Satanic. I touched one of the metal pitchers, tilted it. It was heavy and filled with water. I liked the whole service.

"After the service there was a small train coming outside the house. I had to teach courage to the guy I was with. I dropped to one knee, with knife in hand, a Kung Fu movement called 'Crossing the Bridge.' People rode on the train down the track, faces in the dark. We had to slash across the faces as they came. We did it. Now I knew evil, and helped him understand it also."

A number of weeks before, Joe had puffed himself up and told me proudly, "I could be a criminal. I really know evil!"

Although I did not say so, I doubted his knowledge of evil. He was gripped by it sometimes but was not conscious of it, not even of his own shadow. Now, in the dream, he takes part in an initiation ritual whose purpose is to accept and integrate a piece of collective Jewish shadow, in the service of wholeness. The water of the unconscious gives the ritual its specific character.

Perfection, not wholeness, is the explicit or implicit goal of many spiritual systems as well as most approaches to psychotherapy. Work with the unconscious moves in quite different directions. To reclaim the unconscious parts of oneself, including what is unacceptable, serves wholeness rather than perfection. A person may appear to darken as a result of this process, becoming less perfect but more real, more substantial and human.

Why would anyone want to look flawed? The personal reason is that human beings *are* flawed, and denial does not change the facts. On the contrary, trying to preserve an unreal image amounts to an identification with the gods that merely gives the shadow license to do its dirty work in hidden ways. When we can see and claim the darkness that belongs to us instead of letting it affect the world around us unconsciously, we preserve the dignity of the human condition.

From a social perspective, whoever fails to carry her rightful portion of the psyche leaves it for someone else. In a given environment, some people may look like paragons while others are unconsciously delegated to carry the shadow. If you look closely at someone whose image is unusually bright, you may discover that he is surrounded by scapegoats, shadow carriers who appear to be responsible for the problems in his life. Similarly, many families have one seriously disturbed member who carries the shadow side of the family psychology while everyone else seems to be free of problems. It has been observed repeatedly that when a disturbed child begins to get well, pathology or undesirable behavior may erupt in a brother or sister or parent. That is the moment when the child is likely to be removed abruptly from therapy and returned to the position of shadow carrier, because other members of the family are not prepared to take on their own shadow burdens.

Many of our worst social ills result from the failure to carry shadow consciously. For instance, as nations and races we give away shadow to other nations and races, then go to war against them in a futile attempt to murder the characteristics we cannot bear to see in ourselves. A random mass shooting has a related but somewhat different dynamic, when some unfortunate shadow carrier acts out the unacknowledged murderer in the hearts of a whole community. Such a person lacks even a notion of what compels him to begin shooting.

Joe's inability to accept the Jewish shadow "success in business" kept him from moving about in the world and successfully cultivating his own gifts. This dream asks him, in the name of wholeness, to integrate success in business with the help of a ritual circumcision, a ceremony wherein a sexual token of the unconscious natural man is sacrificed to the Jewish God, affirming that the initiant does not worship the Great Goddess but will henceforth follow a male god. Only by accepting the shadow consciously can Joe "cross the bridge" into manhood. To do it he has to teach courage to the fearful companion who surely embodies his own lack of courage, and sacrifice the "faces in the dark," the side of him that wants to continue to be invisible, carried anonymously along the collective track.

Who is the one behind him, the man with a stick, dealt with so summarily at the dream's beginning? Joe said, "That man had problems. Whenever he'd leave home, when he came back there'd be problems because he'd left."

I can only guess that the man personifies the issue with which the initiation is involved. He is the one who remains his parents' child and cannot move freely between home and the world because he has not been initiated. Like the Nazi and the three-hundred-pound sadist, this man is very threatening. He carries a big stick. Despite having artificially cut family ties, Joe is trapped in the psychology of his family and the problem follows close behind him, interfering with his ability to function in the world.

A month later, Joe permitted himself a small piece of "success in business." He applied for his first change in job status in seven years, to a different department of the store, with higher pay and better working conditions. I was momentarily elated. Then he dreamed:

"I went into a butcher shop and asked for some lamb chops. The butcher turned around and began to cut up a lamb. He kept cutting and cutting, then turned around and handed me the lamb. I asked, 'What's the price?' He said, '$36.' I was outraged. It was too much, not really worth it. I got very angry. I asked him if he could put half of it back. He said no. That was ridiculous. He had just cut up the whole damn lamb, without ever stopping to ask me if it was enough. Then I was thinking, 'Well, I could just walk out without paying.'"

For the first time Joe's dreams bring in a masculine spiritual authority: the *schochet,* the ritual butcher, who tells Joe that something is required of him, something more than he wants to give. It is as if he had walked into a shop and said, "Give me a little humility," and been told, "There's no such thing as a little humility. You either take the whole thing or none at all."

Lamb reminded Joe of the sacrificial lamb. As a child, he had become the sacrificial victim of his father's power drive. He developed the mechanism of burying his talents and feelings to escape that position, but in so doing he cut off his nose to spite his face and put himself even more firmly in the position of the sacrificed one. As an adult capable of carrying his own shadow rather than Max's, Joe no longer has to hide his gifts. Instead of unconsciously being the sacrificial lamb, he is asked to make a conscious sacrifice. He must buy and eat the problem of the lamb, pay for it, cook it, chew it up, swallow it and integrate it. That is, he has to understand the neurotic pattern of sacrifice to which his family psychology drove him, give it up, and instead submit voluntarily to the requirements of his own nature.

When he requested a job transfer, Joe bought as much lamb as he thought he could afford. He stopped pretending to lack sensitivity and talent, and asked for work a tiny bit more commensurate with his nature. Much more is required, however. He admitted to me that in the dream he had enough money in his pocket to pay for the whole lamb, but wanted to keep it for himself. Evidently he has the capacity to pay what his inner spiritual authority requires, but the ego does not want to submit. He would rather walk out without paying.

What is the meaning of $36, the price that Joe so adamantly resists? Numbers in dreams often have qualitative, symbolic meaning unrelated to their quantitative, mathematical properties. Joe told me that numerologically thirty-six is him, his name. From this perspective we can see that Joe has innocently walked into a process of development that wants all of him, no less than total commitment.

A different approach to number symbolism is found in alchemy, where thirty-six might be seen as six times six, the number six intensified. For the alchemists, six signified the attraction between male and female. Knowing this, I wondered if fear of his feelings toward me might lie behind Joe's resistance to paying. His process now demands that he be "cooked" in the intensity of the sexuality between us, an objective, impersonal force that neither of us wants. For the moment, I am the worldly representative of his feminine soul, the part of his innermost being that longs to be united with him. He has met her through our work, but she wants to be still closer. To satisfy her, he would have to bear the sexual tension as an inner/spiritual initiation rather than living it as an outer-world love relationship.

For years Joe has run from one therapist to another, restlessly looking for something. Now he has found it and is engaged in spite of himself. In a manner of speaking, the psyche has him by the balls and wants him to support his feelings with a conscious commitment instead of burying them. True to his neurosis, however, he wants out. He only asked for a *little* something. He does not want what has been handed him, and he will not pay.

Joe's early years had undermined him so badly that he dared not give himself wholeheartedly to any relationship. The psyche's request for total commitment in therapy terrified him because it would bring up childhood dependency feelings, and childhood was a dangerous time. People with histories of severe abuse frequently keep a second therapist in the wings, to whom they flee as soon as they begin to feel dependent on the first. They will understandably go to any lengths to avoid the vulnerability of commitment, but deep healing cannot take place without it.

When I inquired, delicately, if Joe's feelings toward me were a problem to him, he denied having any feelings toward me at all. I was his analyst, he said. Period.

I was puzzled. My vulva told a different story. It is rare for me to feel intense sexual arousal when nothing of the sort is going on in the other person. Still, it can happen. Not wanting to risk attributing something to Joe that might belong entirely to me, I dropped the question.

Two weeks later he dreamed:

"A dentist was doing a surgical operation on my eyes. He put ice on my eyes to kill the pain. I wasn't unconscious. He was cutting carefully around the edge of my eyes with little scissors, to open up my eyes. Then he scraped all the crud off my eyes. He was incredibly skilled, efficient and competent, and used all the latest in dental techniques. I was concerned about losing my sight because of such a delicate operation, but realized that he really knew his stuff."

The operation reminded Joe of a circumcision. He called it "a different kind of briss," but I felt uneasy. On the face of it, it seemed like a good idea to "have his eyes opened," but this initiation is no initiation.

No sooner does the butcher tell him that something is required of him than he flees, putting himself instead into a situation where he can be passive. The operation is done *to* him, without his participation. It takes place entirely in consciousness, contrasting sharply with our work, which involves the unconscious as an equal partner. There is danger that the icy, impersonal technique will destroy his vision, modern and painless though it is. In light of the lamb dream, something is too easy, too clean to be real, entirely too reminiscent of insect spray and aspirin.

My misgivings were vague and I could not articulate them, but I mistrusted the new development and suspected that Joe was looking for an easier way. Later he confirmed it. The day before this dream he had gone to see a former therapist, a man who predated Dr. Kraft.

Joe came to his next appointment "determined to chuck all this." He was in a terrible temper and would have preferred not to speak to me at all, but he wanted to tell me one more dream before he left:

"I was in a shop. There were some Stradivarius violins on the wall, and others were hidden. The owner of the shop, an old guy with grey hair, had put very cheap prices on them, like $86.95, because there was someone who would try to steal them and he thought this was one way of preventing it. The thief came in and a large plastic sheath came down from the ceiling and trapped him."

Stradivarius violins! The most treasured instruments, hidden away, unused and devalued! Joe's abandoned violin lessons prefigured the lifelong suppression of all his passions. I grieved for lost ecstasies, the depths of emotion so incomparably expressed by violins that might never see the light of day.

Who is the thief? Joe said it looked just like *him*. He wants to retrieve his hidden capacities for life and love, to steal them away from the "old guy" who looks like his father, an exploitative patriarchal perspective that locks them up and undervalues them. As the thief he is stopped, however, sheathed in plastic like a depotentiated knife. The violins are "eighty-sixed" to keep them from coming into play. In restaurant slang, eighty-six means putting an end to something. He will end the analysis prematurely and artificially to avoid having to deal with his emotions.

After we talked about the dream Joe said he wanted to continue our work. The next day he called to tell me he had changed his mind. I recognized the voice on the telephone as the one I had first heard seven months before: belligerent, disconnected, vaguely evil. Unable to do otherwise, I accepted his termination of the analysis.

The next week he showed up at his usual hour. I had not filled the time, and willingly made myself available to him. He was pale and frightened. He had just torn his girlfriend Ruth's apartment to bits, pulled her telephone out of the wall, then fled to my office. Superman had taken him over and was throwing his weight around.

The next two months were a nightmare. Previous attacks were pale compared with what assaulted me now. Every week Joe was a little more possessed, but at the same time he clung to me, rapidly alternating between dependency and attack. He asked for extra hours, then used them to berate me and failed to show up for regularly scheduled appointments. He telephoned several times a week, sometimes to attack me, sometimes to ask for help. I struggled to keep my head above water, trying not to fall under the power of what possessed him but to relate to the human being behind it. It became increasingly difficult. He dreamed:

"I was with Lucifer. He was like a goat, like Pan. Then there was a beautiful, Greek-Orthodox Christ, innocent, almost boyish. I was talking to Lucifer, trying to tell him to let me go. He wasn't going to let me go. I kept switching back and forth to where I dug where he was at."

Lucifer, the rejected brother of Christ, was cast out of heaven for his arrogance. In Joe's dream he is like Pan, a nature god, standing in stark contrast to the image of Christ, the willing sacrificial lamb. Identification with either of these archetypal figures is insanity. In refusing the necessary human act of sacrifice, Joe becomes possessed by the dark side of God, the power of nature in its raw form. He alternately likes it and wants to be free of it.

As Joe's possession became more complete, I began to feel as if I were facing the devil himself and found myself shaking uncontrollably before our meetings. Gradually all traces of the human left him. He was quite mad.

Remembering the promise of healing in the image of the double serpent, I tried to hang in there with Joe. One day I fell into a fantasy in which I met the snake from my own dream and was bitten by it. Afterward I was overcome by fear, waves of terror vaster and more intense than anything I have felt before or since. Dimly I knew that the snake's poison was in my blood. I went to bed and lay under the blankets, trembling and drenched in sweat for three days and three nights. After that I was calm. Having lived through it, I knew that nothing would ever again be able to shake me quite so badly.

At that time I did not know that the bite of a poisonous snake is part of the shaman's initiation in some traditions. An initiate who can survive the snake's poison and withstand the ensuing process is protected and prepared to understand and support the healing of others. I see now that Joe served my own initiation far better than the civilized training program in which I was formally enrolled. Then, however, I had no words for what had happened. I only knew that I was stronger than before, and had seen more than I yet understood of the power of another reality.

At our next meeting Joe ranted that he wanted me to give him the secret of the universe, which he imagined I had and was willfully withholding.

"Tell me the *source* of the psychic forces," he screamed, "then I can control them!" His voice fell to a whisper. "Never mind. I *have* the key. The key to get back into the Garden of Eden. Shall I use it?"

Wanting to crawl into a corner and disappear, I got quieter and quieter. As the hour came to an end Joe said, "We'll set up a contest. For you it all hangs on the dreams. Well, I can control my dreams. Let's make a bet. I bet I can make my dreams get *good*. How about it?"

I did not take the bet. I had nothing to say.

The awesome eruption continued for two more sessions. Near the end of the first, I heard my son Nick come home from fourth grade, on schedule, and go into his room. A few minutes later, the most godawful screams reverberated through the house. I ran to Nick's room and found him on the floor having a tantrum. When I was able to calm him, he had no idea why he was screaming. So far as he could tell me, nothing had happened to upset him. Nick usually avoided strong emotions and had never before had a tantrum. Even though he could not have heard it through ordinary sensory channels, I guessed that Joe's insanity had somehow found a way to touch Nick and compel him to scream until his mother came running.

The next week I too was infected. A volcano exploded in the center of my being and I could tolerate Joe's raving no longer. Fury matched fury, abuse matched abuse. Rage consumed me and I gave him back with interest every "fuck" and "cunt" he had hurled at me during those chaotic weeks.

It was his turn to fall into silence. His eyes grew round. I had been angry with him before, but he had never heard me swear. He swallowed several times, blinked, and his mouth fell open. Finally he said, "You shouldn't do that!" Exactly nine months after our first meeting he walked out. Without paying.

6

A Fragile Covenant

When it cooled enough to permit reflection, I was amazed at the depth and tenacity of the rage that Joe's madness had activated in me. Cannily, he did not show up for his next appointment. My control analyst suggested that I drop him a note, but I refused. I did not want to deal with the painful emotions he aroused, and was determined not to see him again under any circumstances. To protect myself from the temptation to let him in should he ever appear at his usual hour, I gave the time to another patient. Whether or not I passed my examination ceased to be of more than passing concern.

Joe had chipped away at my ego for many months, challenging me at every turn, and I had managed to stay more or less rational. What I experienced now came from a wrathful, vengeful place I had not known before. I felt as if some ultimate value had been violated. If Joe in his madness was identified with Lucifer, I was taken over by something akin to Yahweh, the God of the Jews raging at Joe through me.

One evening a friend and I decided to have dinner at a downtown restaurant. Blithely driving my tiny yellow sportscar eighty miles an hour in the fast lane of the Santa Monica Freeway, I could hardly believe it when someone bumped me from behind. I kept going, watching the battered Chevrolet behind me in my rearview mirror. It hit me a second time, and yet a third. Struggling to keep control of my car, I moved a lane to the right. When the Chevrolet sped past, my friend wrote down its license number. At the next exit I left the freeway and called the police. I felt lucky to be alive.

The California Department of Motor Vehicles had no record of the Chevrolet. I was shocked. How could it be? Except for speeding, which I told myself *everyone* did, I had done everything right. I

raged against the unfairness of life, but finally had to accept that I had
no recourse. I dreamed:

"A large, spherical object from above has dropped on my car and
demolished it. Fortunately I wasn't in the car when it happened. I
look at it and throw up my hands saying, 'totaled!'"

Sobered, I reflected upon the event and the dream. I had bought
my car impulsively soon after my divorce, and it seemed to embody a
cocky, fuck-you-all way of getting around in the world that overlooked a certain amount of psychological truth. Through the car I
symbolically thumbed my nose at my former husband and the life I
had lived with him, saying "Nyah nyah, I don't care! It doesn't matter that you abandoned me, because I can take care of myself." It was
a monumental defensive lie that denied my love for him and the pain
and guilt I felt that he had left me. In truth the car, like me, was small
and vulnerable, easily hurt in spite of its sharp, smart-ass exterior. It
was remarkably similar to the statement Joe made by walking away
from his work with me.

Apparently this attitude had incurred the displeasure of a higher
perspective than my own, and had become the victim of the wrath of
God. From the dream's point of view, the only thing that had saved
my life was the fact that I had not been *in* the car when it was hit.
That is to say, I had a little distance from the state of mind the car
represented and was no longer identified with it.

Now I could see why Joe made me so angry. Since I shared with
him the tendency to deny my feelings when I was afraid they might
be misused, I wanted desperately to heal in him what needed healing
in myself. Just as divine rage poured upon Joe through me, so was
the Chevrolet an instrument of superhuman wrath that hit my car like
a "spherical object from above." Something in both of us wanted to
destroy the stupid defense of denying our feelings.

When that became clear, my anger dissolved. I found myself
wondering, and caring, how Joe was getting along. That very day he
called me. He was subdued and hesitant:

"Uhh . . . I took a little vacation. Could I have an appointment?"

I gave him one without comment.

It was no surprise that he contacted me exactly when he did, not a moment sooner or later than I was ready to receive him. Beginning with our two snake dreams, synchronistic events in our relationship were commonplace. It was as if we lived together in the same psychological space, where each could hear and see what was going on in the other, even without physical contact. Since that time I have experienced the same depth of connection with many patients and some close friends. I become increasingly aware that two psyches can become linked like a pair of gears driving a deep healing process that often seems to be set in motion by working with dreams. Once activated, the process goes its autonomous way without regard for the conscious intent of the people who carry it, as if it had its own goals.

Today psychotherapists use the terms "transference" and "countertransference" to talk about many aspects of the relationship between therapist and patient, but the word transference originally referred to a phenomenon like the one I am describing. A patient's sickness was said to be *transferred* directly to the therapist, who then healed it within himself. Contemporary psychotherapy believes that it is always the therapist who heals the patient. Ideally that would be so, but often it is not. When two psyches become linked in a healing way, whoever understands and relates more deeply to the healing process bears the major portion of its burden. Sometimes the therapist carries the full responsibility, sometimes the patient does, and often the therapeutic relationship divides it between them. In any case, this kind of work repeatedly opens a therapist's psychological wounds, healing them over and over again at ever deeper levels. If she tries to cut herself off from her vulnerability, she loses the ability to help her patients and may even do them harm.

When Joe came for his appointment I almost expected to hear that his car had been damaged like mine. It had not, but he had had this dream the night before:

"I was driving my car, with Ruth and her son in the back seat. We had been on a trip and were now returning. When we set out on the trip I had purposely disconnected the radiator gauge so it wouldn't register. I wanted to make the heat go up just a little. I intended to keep it within limits.

"Now that we were coming back I reconnected the gauge and it immediately shot up to overload. It had overheated while the gauge was disconnected. Then it began to cool down right away. I wondered whether the engine had been damaged, but it seemed okay.

"We drove down into a crowded street, teeming with people, and I pulled off and parked to let the car cool off. We got out and there was a beautiful cool breeze in the air. The sun was just setting."

"Joe," I said, "if you don't watch out you're going to crack your block!"

I wondered if he had any idea how overheated *my* engine had been and hoped that now, with the approach of nightfall and a cooling breeze, our work together could be more human.

The week before, Joe had had the dream that drove him to call me again:

"There were insects all around. They looked like large mosquitos. I was trying to get rid of them, trying to smash them with a pillow. Then the whole sky was full of them.

"I went into a screened restaurant to get away from them. A couple of insects came into the restaurant with me. Watching from the restaurant I saw them form into a whirling cloud in the sky, a funnel like a tornado. They thunderbolted through a building with enormous power and speed. They left holes in buildings. Businesses were closed because of the insects."

The ignored and rejected spirit loses the harmless beauty of dragonflies, becoming angry, stinging, and enormously powerful. When Joe tries to kill it with the pillow of comfortable unconsciousness he only makes matters worse. The whole sky fills with insects, threatening a psychosis that could totally blot out the light of day.

The dream reminded me of a passage from the Book of Job where the anger of the Jewish God, the very anger by which I had felt myself possessed, takes the form of a whirlwind:

"Then the Lord answered Job out of the whirlwind, and said, Who *is* this that darkeneth counsel by words without knowledge? Gird up now thy loins like a man; for I will demand of thee, and answer thou me."[1]

Joe thinks he can walk away from the process he has entered, but something in him is like the Old Testament God, compelling him to come back to himself over and over again.

Joe thought the restaurant in the dream referred to our analytic work. Some of the angry insects come into it with him, but he is relatively safe there. From the vantage point of our work, the previously chaotic invasion takes form and becomes a God image, or what Jung calls the Self, the hypothetically integrated whole person. Because they represent an ideal that is never fully achieved, Self images are experienced as very much larger and more powerful than the person knows himself to be. In Joe's psyche, the Self insists that he must keep growing to become the person he was meant to be and live up to the potential with which he was born.

In the form of a tornado of insects, the God image has tremendous power and appears to have purpose and direction, behaving as if it "wants" to destroy concrete and steel buildings. It speaks in the voice of the big dream that has something to say to all of us. Maybe it wants to demolish our materialistic achievements, the puny technological structures we have built on earth without regard for the needs of spirit or nature; or perhaps it only wants to demonstrate its power. Surely Joe's plastic covering, his insect spray and aspirin, his marvelously skilled dentist, even his Nazis and three-hundred-pound man, will not be able to free him from the raw power of the Self. Success in business is not enough. Something infinitely more important is at stake.

---

[1] Job 38:1-3, King James Version.

Between sessions, what we talked about during our weekly meetings tended to become distorted in Joe's mind. He began to tape our
hours in order to listen again and hear what really happened. It
helped. For the time being the work went smoothly.

One day he came in looking miserable. He said there was something he had to talk to me about, even though it made him uncomfortable. Mentally I prepared to receive a confession. Joe said he had
an obsession from which he knew he had to free himself, but he did
not know how and needed my help to work it out. For years he had
gone to one shrink after another, looking for a shaman. Now, in our
work, he felt he had found it. He knew it was sick and wrong. What
could he do to get over it?

I was dumbfounded! I asked, "Why do you think it's wrong?"

"Isn't it?" He was as surprised as I.

I told him I felt the shamanic perspective was a legitimate part of
our work, even a crucial one. He wept.

The psyche brings its own images to the analyst's role: doctor,
teacher, lover, friend, priest, shaman. Our task is not to criticize the
particular archetypal model that imposes itself upon an analytic relationship, but to understand and relate to it in a way that will facilitate
its healing power. Joe was the first to make me aware of shamanic
overtones in my work, and he unknowingly set in motion in my psyche a long and arduous process, whose content I could only understand in the light of shamanic initiation imagery. He never explained
why he thought it wrong to seek a shaman. I imagine the criticism
came from another therapist. Joe's psyche wanted a shaman, however, whether or not anyone approved, and acceptance of that image
for our work brought him some peace. Perhaps so-called primitive
levels of the psyche are required to heal the split between the
archetypes of good and evil, a split that runs like an earthquake fault
through the whole of Western civilization. Images of Christ and Lucifer, for example, express opposites that are sharply separated in
Judeo-Christian culture but can live together in a tribal culture em-
bracing everything that walks on the earth.

A week later Joe dreamed:

"Ruth and I are building a miniature house out of natural wood bark. It is a memorial. I had inherited a memorial to all the Jewish dead."

The tiny bark house contains Joe's spirit in a natural way. Like a Native American dwelling, it belongs to the earth where he lives, but at the same time it is a memorial to the Jewish dead, giving access to his repressed religious roots. Unexpectedly, shamanism reconnects him with the Judaism the Nazi shadow killed so long ago.

For the first time Joe could discuss his Jewish heritage without an outburst of antisemitism. During this time his father called him and they had their first friendly visit in several years. Joe began to read about Judaism. He dreamed:

"Me and a lot of other people were on a ship. Previously all the people had fallen into the icy-cold water and almost drowned and frozen to death. They were saying, 'No more of this journey!' I had to mediate between them and the captain.

"Then the captain spoke. He said we'd just gone through some very dangerous straits. What had happened then would never happen again. We were headed for new waters. What was done was done. The reason for the disaster was the treacherous waters.

"Suddenly in the distance, just above the horizon, the sky was *awesome,* filled with incredible colors. As I watched, an island began rising up out of the water near the horizon. It was a very ancient island, but very advanced too. This was where we were going next."

I breathed a sigh of relief. The end of the dream reminded me of the rainbow in Genesis that signifies God's promise never again to flood the earth and destroy human consciousness:

"And God said, This is the token of the covenant which I make between me and you and every living creature that is with you, for perpetual generations: I do set my bow in the cloud, and it shall be for a token of a covenant between me and the earth, that the bow shall be seen in the cloud: And I will remember my covenant, which is between me and you and every living creature of all flesh: and the waters shall no more become a flood to destroy all flesh."[2]

With the emergence of solid earth from the treacherous waters we had traveled, I felt that the danger of psychosis was past. Furthermore, Joe had accepted responsibility for mediating between the captain, the higher masculine spiritual authority who knew the way, and the forces within him who kept wanting to abandon ship. Finally, the dream reassured us both that we would not have to reexperience the particular disaster we had recently been through. The danger of drowning in icy waters was over. Joe's initiation completed, his masculine strength was secure enough that he could begin to let himself be seen as he was, with his real passion and warmth. He dreamed:

"I was in a locker room changing to go swimming. There were a lot of people there, women and girls as well as men. We were all naked. I noticed my penis. It was of comparative stature with others. It was okay if someone looked!"

Because it reduced his fear of being overwhelmed, Joe's increased masculine confidence permitted him to approach the feminine in a more human way and made it easier for me to work with him. During this time he made three important changes in his life. At the department store he asked for and was given what he called "white man's hours," he found an apartment he liked and moved into it, and he signed up for a class on shamanism at City College. Each new step made him extremely anxious, but each was a little easier than the last, and they all made him feel better about himself.

On his birthday, soon after beginning the class, Joe dreamed:

"I was walking on the moon. There were a lot of men there, scientists, busy exploring. I looked up at the sky. It was divided in two parts, dark on the left (night side), light on the right (day side). Above where I was standing was a bluish-grey streak that separated them. I was aware of the roundness of the moon.

---

2 Genesis 9:12-15, King James Version.

"I looked down again at the asphalt. I was afraid to look up too much—it was just awesome. I was thinking about how I was one of the first men in history to be on the moon. I flashed back to the fathers of Judaism, then back for all time. I had the feeling that if I died, me being on the moon would mean something.

"Then I looked up to the sky again and saw the stars, flame-colored, fiery orange. The sky was absolutely clear, no clouds. The constellations were different than on earth. One was just six stars making a long rectangle. Even that I had to look at out of the corner of my eye. It was too awesome. I felt almost panic. I wanted to get back to my car. Ruth was waiting there. I called to her, almost overcome by it all."

In the outside world, astronauts had landed on the moon four years earlier. I was distressed when I first heard of the plan because I thought that when the moon became concretely known, the mythic moon of poetry and imagination would be destroyed. At the moment when the landing took place, however, my inner image of the moon spontaneously split into two moons and I was filled with relief, for I saw that the mythic moon could continue to exist alongside the known, physical moon. In fact, outer moon exploration may have been necessary before the nature of the inner feminine, heretofore projected comfortably into the sky, could begin to be widely known in the human psyche. As the outer moon becomes better known from a scientific point of view, more and more people are taking the journey Joe took, to explore the ever-changing facets of the mysterious moon within.

I wondered why Joe's moon was covered with asphalt. He told me it was like the asphalt parking lots at City College. For him, taking a university class had the dimensions of a trip to the moon and was just as overwhelming. But in risking the classroom exploration of shamanism he began also to understand the feminine soul, which the alchemists said "has a spherical nature after the likeness of the globe of the moon."[3]

---

[3] Quoted in C.G. Jung, *Mysterium Coniunctionis*, CW 14, par. 167.

As two-faced as Mercury, the inner woman has her night side and her day side. In the dream, Joe wisely stands in the narrow path where her light and dark aspects meet and moderate each other. The moon's mediating position between heaven and earth may make it possible for Joe to look at the spectacular heavens, the activated archetypes, without being blown apart. The sight is too awesome to confront head-on, but he makes good use of his feminine nature when he looks obliquely, out of the corner of his eye. He is almost overwhelmed even then, and hurries back to the familiar, earthly protection of car and girlfriend.

The scientists on the moon embody Joe's newfound ability to bring objectivity to his process of discovery. It is the first time that his dreams have represented the capacities of science in an integrated and nonviolative way. The scientists are simply looking to see what is there, not trying to destroy anything. In that moment Joe experiences the importance and meaning of his individual life in the context of his heritage, extending back through all time.

This time the number six appears in a clearly defined constellation. Even though it takes the impersonal form of a rectangle, he still finds the attraction between male and female symbolized by the number too overwhelming to view directly. In a dream two weeks later, however:

"I was opening some curtains, and suddenly realized that you have become as important to me as Dr. Kraft once was."

For the first time he can let his feelings be, and in the next dream wonderful things are revealed:

"It was dark. I was looking up in the sky. Some falling stars flashed through the sky. Then I saw a long path of stars. There were just incredible things going on in the heavens. I thought of the moon dream, thinking that now it was coming true. I wondered if we would survive, or if this was the end of the world.

"Then I was with a thirteen- or fourteen-year-old girl, very attractive. I was telling her to look at what was happening in the heavens.

She was frightened and kept her eyes shut. I was yelling at her to open her eyes and *look.* Finally she did.

"It was a special night, the beginning of a new era. This point in time would be recorded in history books and could be referred back to as the start of something new. I kissed the girl, and the kiss consummated it."

Finally he makes contact with his lady, the soul image abandoned in early adolescence. Born into the earthly world as a young girl, the moon has become human. *She* is the side of him who is afraid, and he has to reassure her before she will open her eyes and see the wonderful things that are happening.

Who is she? What are the qualities of the soul image that we all have somewhere inside? For each of us she is a little different, and because she partakes of what is divine within, she is mysterious and cannot be encompassed by a rational box of words. Still, we can say some things about her. The lady sees beyond the ideal of "what ought to be" to the place of exactly how things are, and accepts them, permitting the dirt and darkness of life to exist for the sake of the completeness she values more than perfection.

"After all," she might say, "is not our time composed equally of night and day?"

Like nature itself she is irrational, expressing herself in the emotions and instincts that move us in spite of the dictates of reason. Valuing connection more than power, it is she who makes it possible to relate to our fellow human beings, to the world around us, to the gods, to everything that is. Like the stars and moon, she comes out at night when the clear, discriminating light of the sun is momentarily dimmed, to speak in the poetic, nonliteral imagery of dreams and the irrational voices of fantasy and imagination.

To begin to see through the eyes of the feminine soul, look at the appearance of things in moonlight compared to the light of the sun. The clarity, distinctness and certainty of daylight consciousness is replaced by a softer, more mysterious vision, the night peopled by beings invisible during the clear light of day. Then, too, sometimes the moon is totally dark. The brightest moonlight tonight will shortly become perfect darkness. In the dark of the moon, when only stars are visible, you can sometimes see miraculous things in the heavens, like the ones that occurred the night that Joe kissed his lady.

His kiss was a promise, a fulfillment and a new beginning. I felt a deep commitment in it, but once again I underestimated the power of Joe's insecurity to disrupt the tenuous soul connection.

Traces of Joe's belligerence and defensiveness reappeared. Not wanting to deal with another major eruption I handled him with kid gloves, but my capacity for tender loving care was limited. There came a day when a professional meeting took priority over my evening appointments. Joe had been so touchy that I avoided canceling his session, but asked him to come at six p.m., an hour earlier than usual. He did not show up.

He telephoned as I was walking out the door at seven. He said he was having trouble breathing, had heart palpitations and thought he was going to die. I asked why he had missed his appointment. He adroitly sidestepped the question. When had the symptoms begun, I asked? He told me he went home after work, turned on the television, and was sitting there watching it when he began to gasp for breath. He imagined that someone had given him a bad cigarette!

The symptoms disappeared as we talked. I gave him the telephone number of a physician, the number where I could be reached that evening, and an appointment the next day.

When we met, the love-hate push-pull began again. Its flavor was new, however. He dreamed of naughty children instead of Lucifer or Nazis, and in our sessions he behaved like a child who wants to ask for love but is afraid to. A bratty little boy in a dream put pins in his mouth and threatened to swallow them when he failed to get his way, just as in outer reality Joe tried to manipulate me by verbally abusing himself as if to say, "If you really loved me, you wouldn't let me put myself down."

One day he told me how he felt about me. He said, "Sometimes I'm more attracted to you than I am to my girlfriend. It's going to ruin my relationship with her."

The next week he said: "What if you suddenly decided to terminate me? What would I do?" I did my best to reassure him, without notable success. Then he dropped his bomb.

"I've been seeing Dr. Samuelson."

Dr. Samuelson was the male Jewish analyst he had originally considered seeing instead of me.

I felt as if he had hit me in the solar plexus. Carefully controlling my emotions, I asked why he would do a thing like that. He said he felt it was time to "get in touch with my Jewishness." Dr. Samuelson would be able to teach him about being Jewish. He thought it would be nice to see both of us, Dr. Samuelson one week, me the next. He told me that Dr. Samuelson thought it was a good idea too.

Fortunately the hour was over. My head was spinning. My response was polite, professionally correct and totally unreal. I agreed to share the work with Dr. Samuelson, and Joe and I made an appointment for two weeks hence.

As soon as the door closed behind him I reacted. Get in touch with his Jewishness indeed! What did he think we had been doing all these months, anyway? Why hadn't Dr. Samuelson called me? What was he doing messing around with *my* patient without permission?

Dr. Samuelson was a certified analyst. I imagined it had not occurred to him to discuss this situation with me, a mere training candidate. My feelings were hurt, but I realized I did not own Joe and had no right to prevent him from doing what he wished. Hating the professional tendency to think of patients as pieces of personal property, I was distressed to discover this Nazi-like feeling in myself.

I needed every minute of the two-week interval to put my pain and anger in perspective. The more I brooded about it, the more convinced I became that I was wrong to acquiesce in Joe's time-sharing plan. Finally I saw that I had once again been driving my psychological sportscar. In effect I had said to Joe, "I don't care," when I *did* care very much. By deferring to Dr. Samuelson's greater professional status, I abandoned my feelings and buried what I knew about Joe, effectively recreating his childhood abandonment to his father's power drive.

At our next meeting I told Joe I had changed my mind and was no longer willing to cooperate with Dr. Samuelson in this work.

He was dismayed. *"Why?"*

I said I felt he was trying to avoid the intensity of our relationship and thereby duck the task the psyche had set him. If I went along with his wishes, I would only block his progress.

With dramatic gestures, he cried that he *had* to see Dr. Samuelson because he was just like his beloved old Jewish grandfather. I could not believe what I heard! The echoes of Joe's recent antisemitic pronouncements were still ringing in my ears, and I told him I was not convinced. If he wanted to learn about Judaism he could read, take a class or go to the synagogue. If he wanted to connect with himself, including his Jewishness, he needed to stay here, in the heat of his psychological process.

He raged and argued. I pointed out that he was free to do whatever he chose, but my work with him would be independent of anything he did with Dr. Samuelson. He decided to go on seeing Dr. Samuelson. He dreamed:

"I was in the desert with a group of people. Some guy was leading, looking for water. He saw what looked like an oasis, but I knew it was a mirage. When we got there the water started to vanish. There was a smaller waterhole nearby, with real water in it. I was afraid it might be polluted and wouldn't drink out of it. There was a chain in it that might pollute it. Some of the people would drink from it and die."

He pursues an illusion and knows it! The real stuff comes from an unimpressive source that has a chain in it. Limited and limiting, the water without which he cannot live is like a chain that would bind him to his own nature, his own reality, his own fate. It would not permit him to escape it. The alchemists expressed a similar intuition about the ambivalent nature of the psyche's water when they said, "This stinking water contains everything it needs. . . . [It] kills and vivifies."[4] If Joe were to drink of this water he would die and never be the same again because he would have to become fully himself.

I felt defeated by his pursuit of the mirage, his refusal to drink of the real water. I thought, "You can lead a horse to water . . ."

Joe admitted that he went to Dr. Samuelson because of the dream that I had replaced Dr. Kraft in his affections. He was afraid I would be his master, as Dr. Kraft had been, and he would once again be the sacrificial lamb in a power relationship. I told him I did not want to own him, that my deepest need was to give him back to himself. I said that commitment and love are part of the process of finding your soul.

He was not convinced.

The next week he told me he had stopped seeing Dr. Samuelson. He failed to appear for his next hour with me, too. I knew I would not see him again for a while. Maybe never. I reminded myself that Jung says people will go to any lengths to remain unconscious, but I was depressed anyway.

When he called two months later, Joe sounded human, vulnerable and frightened. His voice was shaking. He said, "There's something I want to tell you. I want you to know you were right about what was going on. I do see it, but I just can't work with it now. I don't have the guts."

I thanked him. It meant a lot to me to hear him say it. We talked a bit, catching up on recent developments in his life. I asked him to remember that the door is open.

He said, "Thank you for hearing me. I wanted you to know."

After we hung up, I cried for a long time.

"And Jacob was left alone; and there wrestled a man with him until the breaking of the day. And when he saw that he prevailed not against him, he touched the hollow of his thigh; and the hollow of

---

4 Quoted in C.G. Jung, *The Practice of Psychotherapy,* CW 16, par. 454.

Jacob's thigh was out of joint, as he wrestled with him. And he said, Let me go, for the day breaketh. And he said, I will not let thee go, except thou bless me."[5]

That year, May 25 was a hot day in Los Angeles. Heat came up from the asphalt in waves, lingering on into the night the way it did on summer days in Michigan when I was a little girl. After dark I left the door open, letting in a breath of air along with the sound of sirens screaming down Wilshire Boulevard a few blocks away. My son Nick and I sat in the living room saying his bedtime prayers.

Outside the door a muffled voice said "Janet!"

I jumped. It said again, *"Janet!"* Then, "Do you have a minute?"

Peering into the dark I saw a pale patch of face. He hissed, "It's Joe."

Nick sensed tension and left for bed without the usual argument.

"Come in Joe." He looked terrible. Sweat stood on his face and he was breathing hard. "Are you all right?"

"No."

My heart beat faster. I made myself act calm, offered him a cup of coffee, and got out cigarettes and ashtrays. All the while I felt myself leaving my body, too scared to be in it. I stayed up close to the ceiling and looked down on the two of us, wondering what was going to happen.

He said, "Thank you. Thank you for letting me in."

We sat in my consulting room and he began to cry. It was different from the way I had seen him cry before. He choked out enormous, painful, wrenching sobs that settled into a downpour of uncontrolled weeping. It made me want to cry too, sorry for both of us, two people trying to find our way in a world of gods and demons.

He kept trying to talk and could not. Finally he just cried, for a whole hour. I listened to the sirens in the hot night and waited, my mind racing.

---

[5] Genesis 32:24-26, King James Version.

It's happened. It's finally happened. He's killed someone and has come to me to confess. Did it have to come to this? Was there anything I could have done to stop it? My God, what will I say to him? What will I do? Are the police after him? Or does no one else know?

Under the circumstances I felt strangely quiet.

The sobbing subsided. He sat humbled, human, naked. He stammered, then began, *"I almost killed someone."*

A surge of relief brought me abruptly back to my body. "Thank God you didn't!"

The story tumbled out of him. A few nights ago his demons had moved in on him in full force. He decided to kill Ruth, made a plan, and was really going to do it. Then he realized he would have to do something to stop himself. First he tried to call me but I was out. He knew he was finally alone with it. He drew a magic circle around his bed, got in it and fought with the demons for hours. He broke their grip, but knew it was not forever, only for now.

He told me he had just begun an art class. He had taken several classes since we last met, and was getting more comfortable with school, but the art class had brought on a new invasion. The teacher said his work was outstanding, but so far Joe had destroyed all of it.

He said, "I could stop the battle by staying in my box and not doing anything. But then I'd be dead."

I told him I was sorry I had missed his call that night, but was relieved to know he had developed the tools and the strength to confront the forces within him.

He said thoughtfully, "It's the first time in my life that no one has come to my rescue, and I've had to deal with them myself. I didn't think I could."

He went on, "I'm still working on the things we talked about. I don't dare come back yet. There's a lot more to assimilate. I'm getting it, gradually. I guess maybe I'm slower than most people."

"No, Joe," I said, "you're not slow. It's been pretty heavy. Come back when you're ready."

7

My Daughter the Doctor

Several years later my father, in the dementia of his dying, would look at me proudly and announce to the nurse attending him, "This woman, my daughter, has earned more advanced degrees than anyone else in the Western Hemisphere." Then I would begin to see the role paternal pride had secretly played in my drive for professional credentials, and to understand my perennial conflict between respectability and authenticity as discord between my father's ambitions for me and a path more fully my own. Now, however, as I moved toward the last steps in my program for certification as an analyst, I was unaware of dissonance between patriarchal standards and my feminine perceptions.

Most of the men and women in my training class at the Jung Institute had written their case studies and successfully completed final examinations about six weeks before Joe's nighttime visit. All my friends were now certified analysts and people began to ask me, "Well Janet, when are *you* going to finish?"

The question made me feel a little retarded, but I knew I was not yet ready to finish. Although the work with Joe was deeply meaningful to me, I had no idea how to write about it, no feeling that I "understood the case" in a way that would be acceptable to the examining board. Several months earlier, a series of strokes had disabled my control analyst who was also a good friend. Depressed and disheartened, I had not asked anyone to help me in his stead, preferring to continue the work alone than to enlist the help of someone new this late in the process. But I felt lonely and insecure in my work with Joe.

I also had a mysterious resistance to joining the professional group and becoming "official." It was so hidden within me that I had no idea it was there, but it effectively stopped me from beginning to write.

On May 28, four days after my last meeting with Joe, I had a peculiar dream:

"I am on an ocean voyage, walking alone on the deck at night. A dark, cloaked figure approaches and beckons me to follow. I am led down, down, down, first down steps, then clanging steel ladders, into the dark and cavelike bowels of the ship. The figure points to a small table in the semidarkness. There are stone objects on it. I think they must be cult objects. Moving closer, I see with a shock that they are phalluses, human in size and shape, but made of stone."

The dream's impact awakened me. I was lying spread-eagle on my back. An inner voice commanded, "Lie still, don't move." Struggling with the wish to roll over, to wake up more completely, I felt one of the stone phalluses enter me and was swept with waves of sexual energy. The voice told me to take off my nightgown. I obeyed and lay naked, burning.

I felt a passage opening from a spot between my eyes down through my throat, breastbone and pelvis. Images began to flow through me so fast I could only watch them pass in a shattering intensity of color and light, abstract figures along with scenes from the whole span of my life, but more real than life had ever been or could ever be. Resisting the desire to masturbate, I climaxed from the power of the vision alone and slept peacefully, without dreams.

In the morning Joe's story was fully formed in my mind, waiting only to be put on paper. Despite a full patient load I wrote in a frenzy, using every spare daytime moment and working far into the nights. Ten days later it was finished. It had written itself. I was still too close to it to read it objectively, and wondered if it were totally mad. The examining board would not meet for five more months, so I put the paper aside, happy to have some time to collect myself and gain perspective.

Late in July I looked at it with fresh eyes. Although some of the attitudes it contained were unconventional, it read well, told Joe's story clearly, and adequately described my understanding of our work. I edited it carefully and began to type a clean copy.

I was finishing the last pages when Joe called and asked for an appointment. With mixed feelings I gave him an hour the following week, afraid that further contact would upset my applecart at this vulnerable moment. Now that the writing was done I had become attached to the idea of being an analyst and did not want to fail. What if my ideas about Joe changed? Would I have to write a different paper? The whole thing made me very uneasy.

Meanwhile, my confidence had already been shaken when, for political reasons, I had contacted Dr. Samuelson and talked with him about Joe. Although Dr. Samuelson was not on the examining committee, he was influential in the professional community and I wanted to have his support. To my dismay, he confronted me with the official attitude toward mental illness. He told me that Joe lacked the ego strength to work with dreams, implying that I had made a serious mistake to work in the way that I did. He said I should have helped Joe turn his back on the unconscious and tried to strengthen his ego defenses as *he* did in *his* work with Joe.

Dr. Samuelson's point of view was and is the prevailing psychological and psychiatric perspective. Failing to understand that the psyche *is* a person's inner truth, the official attitude regards dreams as inherently dangerous and imagines that it is possible to strengthen the ego in artificial ways, without reference to the psyche to which it belongs. The attempt to understand unconscious material is perceived as unsafe.

Now I know clearly what nonsense that is. The official attitude toward mental illness cannot heal it. On the contrary, ego stability and strength come from accepting and integrating unconscious material, particularly the shadow. Dreams are one of the best tools for bringing such material to consciousness.

Like any tool, dreams can be misunderstood or misused in dangerous ways. Unethical, ungrounded and irresponsible therapists are dangerous. Those who encourage patients to abdicate personal responsibility by letting dreams make their decisions are dangerous, as are the ones who manipulate dream material to serve their own power needs. However, it is equally dangerous to try to force someone on the edge of a breakdown to conform to cultural expectations that disregard what is happening in the psyche. It only exaggerates the alienation he already feels, and increases the tension between his innermost truth and who he thinks he is supposed to be. *That* is what precipitates insanity.

These perceptions were dimly formulated intuitions when I was working with Joe. Experience has given me confidence in them, but then I was afraid that the examining board would think I used unforgivably poor judgment to work with Joe's dreams, or worse, that my work had in fact hurt him. Approaching official status thus activated a split that was like an earthquake fault deep within me, empowering what I thought I *should* believe and making me doubt my psychological perceptions. I dreamed:

"I am talking with the chairman of the examining board, in his office high in a huge concrete and steel building on Olympic Boulevard. I am supposed to show a film about Jung and answer questions at a meeting. An earthquake begins, gradually gets bigger and bigger, and the building begins to sway. I wonder how far it can sway without falling down. I'm very frightened."

So it was that my psychological ground was shaking as I began the final phase of my work with Joe. Outwardly I continued to work as I had before, but inwardly I was beset by so much uncertainty that Joe was affected by it.

The dream Joe brought to his appointment foretold an auspicious new beginning:

"I went to a meeting place that was also a restaurant. An attractive girl was sitting to my left. At first she was quiet. Then she asked for a dime for coffee. I was going to pay her bill, then thought no, I'd give her the money instead. I gave her fifty cents.

"She was pregnant. She lay down and I could see her abdomen extended. I'd never seen a pregnant woman before. She was going to have her baby in a few days. If she needed transportation, I wanted to take her."

Joe's attitude has changed dramatically. For the first time in a dream he is willing to give what is asked and more. He supports the anima unconditionally, and offers whatever she needs to facilitate her impending labor. Nine months earlier, not long before he left the analysis because he was afraid of his feelings, a seed had been planted. What began then is now ready to bear fruit.

During the session Joe raised a question he had never before asked me directly: "Janet, do you really feel this is the right way for me?"

I told him I thought he had no choice but to meet the psyche and come to terms with it. Until a few weeks before, I could have said it unequivocally. Now doubts and fears eroded my confidence in the dream's optimistic prognosis. I was under the surveillance of an inner board of officials. The nearer I came to my outer-world examination, the more critical the inner-world examiners became.

Something in Joe's process began to go wrong. I already knew that the unconscious usually mirrors the face that is presented to it, that is, that someone who approaches the psyche with inordinate fear, control, suspicion or hostility is likely to activate its frightening, overwhelming, crazy or otherwise dangerous aspect. Joe had experienced the phenomenon repeatedly. Now *he* had the right attitude, however. It did not occur to me that his unconscious would be adversely affected by the doubts and fears that haunted *me* as I approached official status, but something of the sort seemed to happen. Joe began to have dreams that disturbed me, and the more I worried, the more cause I saw for worry. For example:

"I was in the desert. There was a very old man, like a desert rat. As I looked at him, he'd lose parts of his face. It was an awful sight."

I imagined Dr. Samuelson standing behind me, clucking and muttering: "Poor ego strength. Just *look* at that dream. Get'im out of there *fast*. He needs a *man*, a strong man to hold him together. Masculine archetype is falling apart. Bad stuff. Dangerous, dangerous."

I remembered that the chairman of the examining board had once told me about a psychologist friend of his, shot dead by a crazed patient with poor ego strength. My support of Joe's process deteriorated rapidly, and I decided I would have to do something decisive about his ego strength.

Joe chronically owed me money. Occasionally he would catch up with his bill, but most of the time his payments were a few hundred dollars behind the work. It was all right with me. I needed money, but not badly enough to push him for it. Withholding payment gave him a way to control the situation and to express anger in a relatively harmless way. I assumed he would pay me eventually, for he always settled the account at moments when he felt good about me.

Officially, however, a good therapist is expected to make her patients pay on time. Enforcing prompt payment is supposed to support ego strength, and a therapist who does not insist on prompt payment is said to lack self-respect. Therefore I decided it was important for Joe to bring his bill up to date before my exam. In late September I suddenly stepped out of character to take up the issue with him. Because I was out of tune with my deeper self, I spoke abruptly and abrasively. He looked at me in amazement.

"You stay out of those things," he said. "That's not what you're about." He gave me a little lecture about the point of view he expected me to carry. "We have to stay with the inner, here. It's like praying, tapping into the inner power. When you're in the right place inside, then the outer things will take care of themselves."

He might have been quoting back to me something I had said to him at an earlier time, but he illustrated his point with a dream of his own he had had that week:

"Ruth and I were in the desert. There were dunes forming a large circle. We sat on them, looking into the center. The sand within the circle slowly changed to beautiful, rolling ocean filled with life."

Then I realized how out of tune my change in role was with his delicate birth process. My concern with the bill was badly timed and badly expressed, coming out of my insecurity rather than either his or my legitimate need. Reminding myself that analysts are not gods but only fallible human beings I tried to forgive myself, but it was hard. I reread part of an old letter from a friend:

"How can one keep an analyst, no matter how sensitive, wise and kind, from blundering about in the inner sanctuary mistaking incense for dirt, toys for engines and gods for devils?"

How, indeed, I wondered?

When I went to my car later that day I found its windshield smashed. I supposed that Joe had done it, and asked him about it when he telephoned two days later. He admitted that he was responsible for the damage and said he would pay for it. He was badly shaken. He said, "It takes me over, like a little kid. I can't control it"; and later in the conversation, "You shouldn't have handled the money like that. It was a bad time to bring it up."

As if I didn't know!

He told me that his parents had taken all the money he earned when he had his first job. My unexpected request for payment had brought up his childhood helplessness and rage. I said briskly that he was no longer a child and I would not treat him like one, but inside I was sick at heart at what I had done.

The next day Ruth called to tell me that Joe had beat her up. She had called the police and intended never to see him again. She wanted to warn me that I might also be in danger. I thanked her for her concern.

Joe appeared at my door almost as soon as I hung up the telephone. He knew it was my day off and I would have time for him. He told me what he had done, said he was thinking of killing himself, and wanted to know what I thought about that. I told him his life was his and he would have to decide for himself what to do with it, but if he wanted my personal opinion, I thought suicide was a cop-out. Something needed to die all right, but it had to do with old attitudes, old ways of dealing with things. I doubted that his physical death would solve anything for anyone.

We talked for three hours and I asked him to come back the next day. He did, bringing a dream he had had nine months earlier, written on a sheet of butcher paper in huge, wild handwriting with chaotic sketches to illustrate it:

"I was in a building. Ruth and her son were there. A tremor started. Everybody left the building. I was carrying the kid. The earthquake became stronger and the building collapsed. It fell on a bike. We were on open land. The ground was shaking like all hell was breaking loose. It just didn't stop, seemed to go on and on. Was this a message from God trying to tell us something? It could be the end of all of us. A large building on the other side of the building we left was exploding with tremendous explosions. Even the flak was reaching us. Then the ground started to crack open. I pulled Ruth to one side of the fissure. The ground was still shaking with an incredible force. We were near a chain link fence and I thought we might hold on to that. The earthquake was absolutely awesome. I was thinking of the damage it probably was causing in other parts of the country. All the while I felt secure and not shaken by this incredible earthquake. It was a primal earthquake, and seemed to last a very long time."

I thought about my own recent earthquake dream and realized that something much bigger than Joe's or my personal earth was shaking. Our work together had begun in July, 1972, in the wake of the massive cultural upheaval of the 1960s. It was two years after the shootings at Kent State and barely six weeks into the initial events of Watergate. My own earthquake dream occurred soon after Nixon's resignation from the presidency. Meanwhile, during the year of our work, *Zen and the Art of Motorcycle Maintenance* had been printed and the books of Carlos Castaneda had achieved the status of sacred writings in some circles. All the big public buildings, symbols of a reality that had once seemed immutable, were indeed falling down. As Joe's dream revealed, if there were a safe place for him to be at a time like this it would be in the open, together with his soul, for he knew he was safe as long as he brought his lady with him to one side of the abyss.

At such a time it made little sense to seek security in official attitudes, but seek it I did. For all practical purposes I abandoned Joe's

psyche and ran for the illusory safety of a falling public building. I
wanted the sanction of the authorities in my field, whatever the cost.

It could not have been a coincidence that the closer I got to the official approval I sought, the more completely Joe fell apart. My case
notes during the month before my exam tell the story:

*9/29/74. Joe called to terminate again. He said his need to see me
was compulsive. "I have to withdraw from it. It's the only way to get
over it. It's like a drug."*

*10/3/74. I presented Joe's case at a meeting of the C.G. Jung
Clinic staff. The presentation was wildly successful. I congratulated
myself and anticipated a successful examination.*

*10/5/74. The left-hand door of my car was gouged and scratched,
as if with a screwdriver or a large nail. I made no attempt to confirm
my suspicions about who did it. I did not report the incident to the
police.*

*10/10/74. Joe telephoned. He said, "I have to keep the connection
with you. I don't want to, but I'll go crazy if I don't."*

At this point I offered him undiluted official attitudes. I told him I
wanted to work with him in cooperation with Dr. Goldstein, a psychiatrist on the staff of a local hospital whose medical degree qualified him to prescribe medication. I wanted the doctor, a staunch advocate of the official point of view, to evaluate Joe's condition. At
first Joe was delighted when I asked him to make an appointment
with Dr. Goldstein, hoping at last to have the pair of analyst parents
he thought he wanted. He made an appointment for the following
Monday, but something rang false to him and on Sunday he called
me again.

"What kind of a guy *is* Dr. Goldstein?" he wanted to know.

I tried to reassure him by telling him that Dr. Goldstein was the
kind of person who could give him the help he needed, but I was lying and I imagine he guessed that I had abandoned him. He did not
keep the appointment.

My examination was at eight p.m. on a rainy November evening,
at the Sportsman's Lodge in the San Fernando Valley. There would

be six examiners, three well known to me and three virtual strangers from another city, among them the wife of Martin Cooper, world-renowned analyst.

I drove there alone in my little sportscar and sat trembling in the motel's deserted lobby, waiting to be called. Then Dr. Cooper himself strolled through the front door. When he saw me, he stopped and spoke to me.

"You must be Janet Dallett."

I was startled that he recognized me. He put his finger to his lips and said, "I read your paper. I shouldn't tell you this, but you'll be fine. Don't worry."

Before I could respond he disappeared into a corridor.

With the blessing of the Great Man upon me, how could I fail? I spoke with the voice of a nightingale that night, but my tongue was forked. No one asked how Joe was getting along now. No one even thought to deplore his lack of ego strength. Three hours passed in a blur of collegial congeniality, and at eleven p.m. I was pronounced an analyst.

I did not hear from Joe again.

An ancient proverb says that if you save a person's life, you will be bound to him forever. My work is like that. It cuts so deep that I carry around pieces of some of my patients for years, maybe forever.

When I worked with Joe, his whole psyche was on my back. If he had owned more of himself he could have let me go, but as it was, he was stuck with me and I with him. Paradoxically, owning himself would also have allowed him to stay in the analytic relationship until the work was finished. In the style of Dr. Kraft, he tried to demonstrate his power by cutting me off, acting on the absurd but common belief that a healthy person should be able to do anything he wants. The fact is that life and the world impose limits. Even more so does the psyche. Joe bumped against his psyche's limits whenever he tried to run away from me, not realizing it was himself he wanted to escape. For him, sanity could only come from reconnecting with "her."

So long as he saw me as identical with "her," he could approximate sanity only by staying connected with me.

As for me, I often think about a colleague's comment that analysts are lazy people who rely on our patients to activate the material that forces us to the work of self-understanding. Joe played that role in my life with a vengeance. As is often the case with people who arouse strong emotions in us, he created the opportunity and the necessity for me to go deep into my own unconscious psychology. His tendency to deny his feelings because they made him feel powerless made me aware how often I use the same defense mechanism. The sacrificial lamb in Joe's psyche led me to examine my own scapegoat psychology. His fascination with the shaman archetype activated and illuminated the shamanic aspect of my work. In its own way, my creativity was as immobilized by patriarchal power psychology as Joe's, and working on his material helped me see it. Just as he was relentlessly pursued by something larger than the narrow concerns of daily life, so does my psyche require me to live in relation to the mysterious unknown called God or the Self, the other-worldly realm of spirit and soul, the place of the big dream. Whenever I understand a new piece of that long-ago analytic relationship, it illuminates another facet of my own unconscious.

When I telephoned Joe last year from my home in Seal Harbor, I had no idea what to expect. The possibilities seemed infinite. I imagined he might be dead, insane or in jail. Maybe he would hang up the minute he heard my voice, I thought, or perhaps he would cry. Worse, he might not remember me at all.

Actually, he was pleased to hear from me and sounded healthy and strong. He said he had read some of my published writings, and was taking a psychology course at City College. Most important, he was still chewing on the things that came up in our work, things we had talked about fifteen years before.

"It's not finished yet," he said. "What began then was more powerful and important than I knew. Now I see that I can't escape the psyche. Slowly, slowly, it's all getting integrated."

For me, digging through this material is like trying to make a tunnel through the mountain of sand my father dumped in our yard when I was a very small child. I'm glad Joe is still digging in the sandpile too. Perhaps one day our hands will meet, and we'll both see through to the other side.

8

A Time for Thieves

As soon as I walked into the motel office, the white man running it used me as an excuse to abuse his Indian wife. No matter what she said, he would not stop yelling at her that I probably wanted a cabin instead of the room I asked for and she gave me. I stood there signing the register, thinking about walking out and imagining telling him to be quiet and leave her alone, knowing if I did it would only be worse for her later.

So I bit my lip and when he yelled for the third time, "Maybe she doesn't *want* a motel room," I looked at him like a rattlesnake ready to strike and said in my coldest voice, "Yes I do. I don't want a cabin." It was not what I expected to find on the Quilleute Reservation, out on the Washington coast at the "true ocean," 150 miles from my home on Puget Sound.

It was the true ocean all right. To get to the beach I climbed over massive timbers thrown like giant pickup sticks. When I finally got there, one of the biggest waves I have ever seen rose up from nowhere, way out in the water. I watched it transfixed, as if I didn't know what was going to happen, until icy saltwater boiled up to my waist and I had to hang on hard to the uprooted end of a giant tree not to get pulled out to sea. Then I fought my way back over the logs to motel room #13, which was not a cabin. After my clothes dried, I sat on the porch watching the waves crash every which way, while the east wind blew their tops back like women's long hair. Later, four wild horses came looking for handouts, their coats thick and burred from winter.

The next morning I found a trail to walk in the forest near the reservation. A little way past the parking lot was a sign that had been there a long time, carefully incised on a wooden plaque, in sober Park Service letters:

3rd Beach Trail
Beach 1.3 mi.
Parking lot subject to theft
Are your valuables secure?

I stopped and thought about it for a while, then started to walk again. Further on, just past the co-ed outhouse, the Park Service had put up a second sign. It said:

This path takes you to the edge of the Olympic wilderness.
From a human-shaped world you are about to step
into terrain dominated by other forces.

I stood there perplexed, reading it over and over to be sure it said what I thought it did. There was a sound and I looked around uneasily before I realized it had begun to rain, the slow, steady drizzle of the Olympic Peninsula. I went on, pondering:

This is the borderland. Here spirit and nature intersect the human world, wiping out our fantasies of superhuman power, childish scratchings on the cosmic blackboard.

Native People know that only gods can be perfect. Whatever man or woman creates must have a human flaw or the soul will become trapped. Native rugs and blankets are made with an irregular thread, a path for the soul to get out. Without it, life would get stuck, unable to move on into the unknown new.

Will we ever learn how to let the soul go free?

This perilous trail through no man's land is the way to human wholeness. Perfection doesn't live here any more. The thieves have come.

When I moved to Seal Harbor it was a little paradise. I never locked my door. There was no need to. Within three years, an epidemic of petty crime had begun. Now the police blotter printed in the *Seal Harbor Advocate* carries half a dozen stories of thievery every week. Wrongdoers tend to be very young. Most are under twenty-five, many younger than eighteen.

Stephen is twenty. He has been stealing since he was twelve, maybe longer, although he did not get caught until he was fifteen. He and his mother Tanya are very close. She has always been a good mother to him. During his years of crime, she has treated him with the same fair, reasonable and knowledgeable attitude with which she raised him.

Stephen is dazed. He has no idea why he steals, over and over again, in spite of the consequences. When his mom talks to him, everything she says is so reasonable he feels she must be right. She is always right. He knows he would not be in such trouble if he had listened to her.

Stephen is haunted by a dream he had when he was a very small child:

"Me and my mom are starting to cross a bridge. Suddenly she leaves. She turns around and goes back the way she came. There is a seal, an enormous bull seal. It comes toward me. I'm terrified. I want my mom. It is going to attack and eat me. I am screaming for my mom."

He has no idea what the dream means. In the outside world his mother has never abandoned him. In the outside world he knows seals rarely attack people. But he remembers the dream and is afraid.

I don't know what it means either, but I have some ideas. Early childhood dreams that are remembered during adulthood often reveal an archetypal structure which, like a skeleton of the psyche, will dominate a person's development throughout life. Stephen's dream hints that he has a fate as big as a bull seal, a very masculine fate already prefigured when he was a small child. When the moment comes for him to separate from his mother and cross into his own life, he wants to stay with her because he is afraid of the initiatory experience. As a result his totem animal, symbolizing a deeply instinctive level of the man he is meant to be, approaches him in an assaultive, destructive way. Because he fails to grow willingly into his masculine identity, it simply takes him over in a negative form that can destroy his life. He is eaten up by the compulsion to steal.

Fate is like that. You cannot escape it, but the particular way in which it affects your life will depend on your attitude toward it. If you are unfriendly to your fate, you will activate its hostile side.

Tanya is well thought of in Seal Harbor. For her sake, Stephen has been given every opportunity to be responsible for his actions and receive a light sentence. The juvenile court was lenient with him, but soon after his eighteenth birthday he ran away from a scheduled appearance in adult court and went to Arizona, looking for a savior in the form of his father. When his father refused to hide him, Stephen realized he was in deep trouble. He telephoned Tanya to talk things over with her. She explained that if he came back to Seal Harbor to face the charges, he might get off fairly easily, even though he had damaged his case by running away.

Stephen was pissed off that Tanya would no longer let him live at home with her and his two sisters, but Tanya's friend Rosemary offered him a room in her home if he would come back and face the music. He decided to follow his mother's advice, and returned to Seal Harbor to live with Rosemary and her two young sons until he was sentenced.

Tanya dreamed:

"A whale has been beached at Seal Harbor. For a long time it looks as if it will die. Then people come and put water on it and talk to it. Eventually there are enough people to begin to move it back into the water. The tide comes up and the people gather around the whale, somehow moving it without touching it. Slowly, slowly, the whale is set free and swims away."

Tanya thought the dream meant that Stephen would not have to go to prison. I thought otherwise. A whale is much bigger than Stephen, Tanya or me. I thought the dream meant that Stephen's trouble is part of a very big trouble in the community, perhaps in the whole culture. I thought it meant that Stephen's thievery embodies an archetypal problem that belongs to you and me as well as him. Stephen has become one of society's scapegoats for trouble in the realm of the human spirit, a problem as big as a beached whale and as masculine as a bull seal.

Swimming in the sea of the psyche, marine mammals emanate a profound sense of potency and grace. In the outside world, their existence has been endangered by a distortion of the masculine spirit, humankind's compulsive greed to steal all the earth's resources and power. We hardly know what it means any more to respect the divinity of life living by its own rules in its own element. Our desire to possess everything leaves the natural life of the spirit high and dry, stuck like a beached whale. It can only be restored to its rightful place when the tide turns and enough people honor it. Then, when the big trouble is put right, life can flow again and perhaps Stephen and others like him will no longer be compelled to steal.

The week that Tanya dreamed of the whale, my friend Elizabeth in Southern California also dreamed a big dream, whose implications reach far beyond her personal psychology into the roots of contemporary life. A startling picture of divine power bequeathed to thieves, it hints at the nature of the archetypal matrix that empowers thievery:

"I am outside a church. A woman friend begs me to go inside with her to say good-by to a teenaged boy who has died and is lying in state. I am reluctant to go in and see his dead body, but go for the sake of my friend. The boy in the coffin is blond and handsome, the embodiment of the young hero. A woman caretaker is there to tend the body. A strapping, muscular teenager, he begins to move. Then he thrashes around, gets out of the coffin and tries to frighten the caretaker. She knows he is in the last throes of death, and is not dangerous. He is moving like this because he was once so vital and young and vigorous, so full of energy, that even in death some life remains in his body.

"Three young thieves are sitting behind us. They are very threatening. They are friends of the dead boy, who now gets back into the coffin and begins disposing of his property. He throws things out of the coffin, one at a time, and each time one of the thieves takes it. We think the women should get something. It doesn't seem right that the thieves should get everything, but there's nothing we can do to stop them."

Elizabeth's dream expresses something of what is happening in this culture as we approach the end of the century and move into the borderland between the old, Christian era and whatever is to come. She is called into the church, the official spiritual container of the passing age, to witness the death of the blond god/hero who is an image of the perfect man, an archetype in the last throes of its death. It is as if she were told, "God is dead," but his possessions, the energy and power of divinity, are passed on to three young thieves in whom the masculine spirit is alive and well. They are intent on keeping it out of the hands of the women.

Caretaken primarily by women, the masculine spirit in this country has been in trouble for several generations. It is like a dead man throwing its weight around. Just as the dream's dying hero is tended by a woman, so most men alive today were raised primarily or exclusively by women. Many spent their formative years with divorced or unmarried mothers. If their mothers worked, women provided day care. An earlier generation had fathers who lived at home but worked away from home and showed little real interest in their sons, leaving the caretaking entirely to mother. When the boys went to school, their first teachers were women. Now grown, these men are quick to acknowledge that they do not know what it means to be a man, nor how to be adequate role models for *their* sons. The cycle then goes on for another generation.

The death of the blond god and subsequent activation of underworld heroes is currently visible in films and other vehicles of popular culture. The Boy Scout type of film hero, characterized by goodness and light, is giving way to the image of the young hood. For most contemporary young people it is the thug who has sex appeal.

There was a time when young men of "good family" were rarely to be found in jail. No more. The young thief is everywhere, underscoring the scarcity of positive adult masculine role models. Few men today can find their connection to maleness in the shining blond hero. That god is almost dead. He has given his power to the thieves, and Stephen has gotten some of it.

It is a dangerous time. The patriarchal archetype upon which Western culture rests has lost its vitality and become unstable. In need of renewal, it has moved into a kind of border space until new god images emerge. It is like a person going through a breakdown. Just as an individual in breakdown becomes something of a psychological outlaw, in whom the culture's boundaries are shattered and whose personal identity is dissolved until it can find its proper shape, so it is now with the dominant archetype. While the blond god completes his death throes and the thief in the psyche gains power, social mores will remain fluid and uncertain. At such a time, only a firm sense of ethical responsibility keeps the individual from petty or larger crime.

The telephone was ringing. I came up fathoms into consciousness and peered at the clock's luminous dial. 12:15.

"Hello?"

Rosemary's voice was muffled. "I'm sorry to bother you at this hour, Janet. I don't know what to do. Stephen is out. The boys went into his room to get a blanket a little while ago. They found a whole bunch of stuff in there. A computer, a camera, some other things I know aren't his. They have Seal Harbor School System inventory numbers on them. He must have stolen them."

My numbed mind tried to reject what it heard. I wanted to go back to sleep. I mumbled something helpless, then realized that Rosemary needed company, even if I had no idea what to do. Hastily I put on some clothes and went to her house. Tanya was there too. The three of us discussed what to do. We decided to wait until Stephen came home, confront him with what had been found and go with him to the police.

The longer we waited the more absurd I found our plight: three women waiting to insist that a young man behave like a man. Where were the men?

We named the men we knew. Rosemary's husband was out of town. Tanya's partner did not get along with Stephen. There was no man in my life then. We thought of friends, community leaders, Stephen's therapist, other therapists.

One at a time we called and asked them to join us in confronting Stephen. One by one the men explained, quite reasonably, why they could not. I began to get angry. What was the matter with these men? What kept their instincts from mobilizing to help the boy? No wonder he was in trouble!

Discouraged and exhausted, we kept trying. Finally Donald, a local counselor, agreed to help. He suggested that we put the stolen items back in Stephen's room and wait until the next day. Stephen's lawyer would be in his office then, and we needed his advice.

When Stephen came home at four a.m., we were all asleep in our beds and he suspected nothing. Later we discovered that he had robbed several stores that night and hidden the loot in Rosemary's shed.

The next day Tanya, Donald and I met Stephen for lunch and told him what we had found in his room. He was enraged with his mother for betraying him. He lied that he was holding the stolen items for someone else. We pointed out that, even if it were true, he was liable as an accessory. He could hear nothing but his rage at his mother. She had never deceived him before, but today she had invited him to lunch and set him up for a confrontation.

We took Stephen to his lawyer, who gave the police the loot we had found without revealing its source. Pending his appearance in court, Stephen continued to live with Rosemary. A week later a police search uncovered many more thousands of dollars worth of stolen goods in Rosemary's house and shed. The next day Stephen was arrested, without possibility of bail. He was enraged. And relieved.

In the Seal Harbor jail, Stephen injured an officer by dropping a pile of encyclopedias on his head. He wore a stolen jacket to court the day he was sentenced to ten years in the state penitentiary. It was Good Friday.

Good Friday. Two days before Easter, the first Sunday after the first full moon after the spring equinox. I got up that morning and put on a bright purple blouse, with a bright green sweatshirt over it. It made me feel good to dress like an Easter egg and think about the timing of the central Christian mystery depending on the pagan moon; to cover the purple of Jesus' martyrdom with green, the color of nature renewing itself.

I thought about Stephen. What a strange coincidence that he would be sentenced on this of all days: Good Friday, when Jesus was hung on a cross to suffer the agonies of the damned, crucified between two thieves.

What became of the thieves? They say that one of them went to hell, but the other was glorified along with Jesus:

"One of the criminals hanging there abused him. 'Are you not the Christ?' he said. 'Save yourself and us as well.' But the other spoke up and rebuked him. 'Have you no fear of God at all?' he said. 'You got the same sentence as he did, but in our case we deserved it: we are paying for what we did. But this man has done nothing wrong.' 'Jesus,' he said, 'remember me when you come into your kingdom.' 'Indeed, I promise you,' he replied, 'today you will be with me in paradise.'"[1]

Two thieves. Unlike the first, the second knew what he had done and was prepared to pay the price. Otherwise they were the same, two thieves in a long and honorable history of thievery, beginning with Adam and Eve. Like the first thief on the cross, Adam failed to acknowledge his responsibility in the little matter of The Apple. When God asked him, "Have you been eating of the tree I forbade you to eat?" Adam pointed to Eve and said, "It was the woman you put with me; she gave me the fruit and I ate it."

Men have been doing that for centuries, blaming their women for the consequences of their own shortcomings. Regrettably, Eve's behavior was none too exemplary either. *She* blamed the serpent.

---

[1] Luke 23:39-43, Jerusalem Bible.

Jesus was different. He was perfect. He accepted his fate and blamed no one, even for the pain of crucifixion, the ultimate self-sacrifice. But he was a man who became a god and lost his earthly status. It took two thieves to balance his perfection. One was utterly unredeemed, but the other had attained a profoundly ethical stance, a new peak of development in the history of the human spirit. He took full responsibility for his shortcomings and paid the price for them, without having to have a scapegoat. In carrying the blame for his thievery, he reached the ethical level of Christ while still remaining human.

When we forget that two thieves are an integral part of the archetype, Christianity becomes distorted and people try to look like gods. We separate ourselves from the human condition and deny our faults because we think we are supposed to be more Christlike than a person can authentically be. Then, in one form or another, the thief creeps in. Sometimes he comes in a dream. Almost as often he manifests in outer reality: the house is robbed, one of the children begins to shoplift or we ourselves are caught by the compulsion to steal.

Victor is a case in point. A brilliant, knowledgeable, eminently reasonable man, he appears to have no faults. Whatever the question, Victor always has an answer. In thirty years, I have never heard him say, "I don't know." Many people see him as a savior and worship him as if he were a god.

Victor preserves his bright daylight image by keeping its black underside hidden. He is a secret thief. When he was accused of questionable financial dealings, he moved abruptly to another state and the charges were dropped. However, he could not avoid an investigation that left him owing many thousands of dollars in back income tax. Some of the expensive equipment in his house belongs to a college for which he worked many years ago. No one seems to notice that he never returned it. Maybe no one cares. We give privileges to our gods that mere humans are denied.

I first began to see perfection's shadow when I discovered that one of my patients had perfect parents. Unlike Victor, they did not just present a perfect image to the world. So far as I could tell, everything they did with respect to their only child was reasonable and right. Elaine, who was then twenty-two and married, would describe childhood events to me and I would say, "And what did your parents do then?" or "What did your mother say when you did that?" expecting to find the usual complement of parental error. Even from the relatively subtle perspective of my psychological training, however, I could find nothing to fault.

Why, then, was Elaine so disturbed? Why was she compelled to beat her head against the wall of the house she occupied with her new husband? I was thoroughly perplexed. Then she had a dream:

"I am with my mom and dad in the garden of the analyst, a stern and fatherlike old man with a white beard. A young apricot tree is growing in a pot near the center of the garden. The analyst and I are talking about the fact that the pot is out of place and the tree has not bloomed yet. We walk in the garden looking at the plants that are in pots. Suddenly I see an insect attached to the leaves of one of the plants. It is lying dormant, but I want to know about it so I poke at it, and it turns into a reptile, a toadlike creature. It begins to devour a mother and her child. It is not limited to time and space any longer, but just fills up the space in front of me. Its neck grows longer and longer until it is like a long, long cord, and the neck and head begin to weave back and forth like a serpent's."

The analyst in Elaine's dream was not me, but a wise old man. He reminded her of Dr. Johns, the clinic director who had initially referred her to me. She felt Dr. Johns to be the very image of God the Father. For the first time I understood that her perfect childhood had been like a Garden of Eden, ruled by the patriarchal god of truth and reason.

In Elaine's garden, however, the serpent that would have initiated her into conscious life had been asleep. Having so little experience of human darkness and imperfection, Elaine became disturbed as soon as she had to live with a real husband in a less than perfect world. Her tree of life was misplaced and had not yet bloomed. So long as it was contained in a pot, it was protected from the difficulties to which she would be exposed if it were planted in the earth. Under these circumstances it/she could grow no larger.

As she discussed the problem with the analyst, Elaine's desire for consciousness aroused the dormant serpent, which began right away to devour the ideal mother-daughter relationship of her childhood. Only then, with the entrance of the thief, could Elaine begin to grow and change.

When control over human nature goes too far, people become too good to be true, too right to be real, too reasonable to be human. The drive for perfection turns into a Nazi, whose compulsive demand that people be gods destroys every trace of humanity. By the time I met Elaine, I had already tried for eight years to be a perfect mother to my son Nick, goaded by guilt after his father and I were divorced. At least once a month, Nick and I lived out a pattern that would begin whenever I felt tired and impatient. Since my perfect-mother ideal would not permit me to show my feelings directly, I became the living image of long-suffering patience. Appearing not to notice, Nick would then do something harmless but annoying, like kicking rhythmically against the leg of a table, talking compulsively or demanding my attention when I was on the telephone. My guard against imperfect emotions would then clamp down even harder.

It went on for days at a time. I played at Paradise by pretending to be better than I am, while Nick, in the role of thieving serpent, found more and more devilish ways to irritate me. When I was finally unable to contain it any longer, my rage would erupt like hot lava and Nick would go off to play, humming quietly to himself, happy as a clam until the next round a few weeks later.

Elaine taught me my lesson. Once I saw that perfect parents are not what they are cracked up to be, I began to let myself be myself, complete with impatience and other human failings. Then life at our house became livable.

Hermes, the ancient Greek god of thieves, had close equivalents in the Roman Mercury, Germanic Wotan and North American Coyote. For all practical purposes, Hermes was born thieving. He crept out of the cradle to steal the cows that belonged to his older brother Apollo, the established sun god of reason, order and light.

Thieving is not the only activity of this elusive, multifaceted god. Among his many functions, he rules over the borderland between one thing and the next, typically appearing during transitional times like the one in which we are now living. He is a shape-changer, one of whose many forms is serpent. As such, he is secret cousin to the serpentine tempter who put an end to Paradise. Just as Adam and Eve lost their comfortable existence in a perfect garden dominated by a perfect god, receiving instead the gift of real lives in the flawed human world, so Apollo lost his comfortable status as property owner, but his life was enriched by the gift of music when Hermes made him a lyre. Thus are we transformed by the chaos and loss the thief creates.

In "The Spirit Mercurius," Jung summarizes "The Spirit in the Bottle," a fairy tale which penetrates deep into the psychological meaning of the Mercurial spirit, the archetypal thief in the contemporary psyche:

"Once upon a time there was a poor woodcutter. He had an only son, whom he wished to send to the university. However, since he could give him only a little money to take with him, it was used up long before the time for the examinations. So the son went home and helped his father with the work in the forest. Once, during the midday rest, he roamed the woods and came to an immense old oak. There he heard a voice calling from the ground, 'Let me out, let me out!' He dug down among the roots of the tree and found a well-sealed glass bottle from which, clearly, the voice had come. He opened it and instantly a spirit rushed out and soon became half as high as the tree. The spirit cried in an awful voice: 'I have had my punishment and I will be revenged! I am the great and mighty spirit Mercurius, and now you shall have your reward. Whoso releases me, him I must strangle.' This made the boy uneasy and, quickly thinking up a trick, he said, 'First I must be sure that you are the same spirit that was shut up in that little bottle.' To prove this, the spirit crept back into the bottle. Then the boy made haste to seal it and the spirit was caught again. But now the spirit promised to reward him richly if the boy would let him out. So he let him out and received as a reward a small piece of rag. The spirit said, 'If you spread one end of this over a wound it will heal, and if you rub steel or iron with the other end it will turn into silver.' Thereupon the boy rubbed his damaged axe with the rag, and the axe turned to silver and he was able to sell it for thousands of dollars. Thus father and son were freed from all worries. The young man could return to his studies, and later, thanks to his rag, he became a famous doctor."[2]

Right at the beginning of the story we are told the conditions under which the thieving spirit is activated: The resources available for the university have dried up. Like Stephen, the hero in our tale can no longer find meaning in the path of reason, order, knowledge and light. In order to renew his resources he has to go back home to the forest, a natural place where achievement is not the dominant power. Here, in deepest nature, he uncovers the mysterious Mercurial spirit. It has been shut away, bottled up in glass and hidden in the roots of a giant tree.

Glass, with its qualities of transparency and rigidity, often symbolizes reason or intellect. Reason bottles up and contains the natural spirit, one of whose forms is human emotion. In Freud's day sexuality was an obvious instance of the bottled-up spirit. In our time, anger is more likely to be repressed. Whatever its specific shape, the spirit buried in each of us speaks of how we really feel and who we really are, in contrast to idealized notions about how we ought to feel and be. By digging deep into inner truth, we can restore the human condition and recover the energy to go on in a new way.

As the tale reveals, however, it is dangerous to set natural energy free when it has been bottled up for a long time. It can become so big that it destroys a person. In this time when the prevalence of child abuse and domestic violence is getting so much public attention, and the threat of nuclear holocaust hangs like a perpetual black cloud, we have ample evidence for the destructive power of the spirit of nature

---

2 *Alchemical Studies,* CW 13, par. 239.

released indiscriminately. The next step is to demonstrate that our ethical sensibilities are sharp enough to get it back under control. Only then can we relate to it safely.

Still, the mercurial spirit is an essential catalyst for healing the problem of the boy in the fairy tale, which is a major problem of our time and the problem that Stephen the thief is carrying. Resources are no longer available to pay for more control, more knowledge, more reason, more light, more righteousness. Perfection is a divine state, not a human one. To heal the deep wounds so many of us bear, we must gain access to the darkness and irrationality of real emotions, humbly grounding ourselves in the flawed human condition that lets the soul go free. The thief is a primary catalyst now, as we step over the boundary of an old age and enter into the new. Ready or not, his time has come.

On a somber Northwest Sunday, Tanya cut her waist-length hair very short and put on black clothes. She searched her house for Stephen's possessions and burned them all, in a ritual act of grief.

Nine months later Stephen was released from the cell he shared with seven other men in the Washington State Prison on McNeil Island. He was moved to a work camp, later to a tightly supervised communal house where he received counseling and an opportunity to look for employment in a town not far from Seal Harbor. The job he found with the State Park Service satisfies his wish to work outdoors, in contact with nature. When he was paroled, his first purchase was a pet snake.

9

If I Were a Golden God

The day I officially became an analyst was the day I glimpsed the depth of Jung's statement, "Thank God I'm Jung and not a Jungian." It was as if others suddenly saw me as a different person, bigger than I had been a mere twenty-four hours earlier, bigger than I was or could ever be. Another member of my training group dreamed that we all climbed into a large hollow statue of a man and fell asleep. I wanted to shout, "Listen! I'm not a Jungian, I'm Janet!"—but it was too late. I had already lost my mortal status.

When I moved to another town ten years later, I began right away to hear rumors that I was a famous European psychiatrist who was in Seal Harbor to "start a center." In truth I was not famous nor European nor a psychiatrist, and had moved precisely to elude organizational entanglements of the kind implied by the words "start a center," but the myth-making power of the psyche is so great that it was hard not to identify with the projected image and live it out.

The lives of people in the public eye are often completely determined by the near-idolatry that results when godlike archetypal images are cast upon human beings. Thus did Marilyn Monroe become goddess of love and Bob Dylan the prophet of a new age. The humanity of therapists and doctors is similarly threatened by the psyche's mythologizing tendency. When we identify with our own fantasies of omnipotence or our patients' wishes that we be savants or saviors, we sacrifice the capacity to be ordinary people living ordinary human lives and, paradoxically, lose the authentic relation to the gods that lies in becoming fully and deeply ourselves.

I imagine that myths originate in much the same way as rumors. Both arise to explain what is unknown, but instead of supplying outer-world facts, they give spontaneous, symbolic expression to psychological truths about the people or culture from which they spring. For instance, the rumors about what I was doing in Seal Harbor said nothing about me but a great deal about the community.

Like many people today, residents of Seal Harbor feel a lack of spiritual life, and are unconsciously looking for a savior to heal personal and communal wounds. Although therapists abound there, most use techniques whose purpose is to make things look better on the outside without going too deeply into wounds or their roots in the psyche. The rumors hint that Seal Harbor has room for something much bigger, something big enough to be famous and different enough to be foreign.

Maybe the hoped-for savior is seen as European because a prophet is without honor in his own land and depth therapy was imported from Europe, or perhaps some people confuse me with Jung. The savior must be a psychiatrist because Seal Harbor has only one psychiatrist, leaving residents without access to a second opinion about medical intervention in psychological disturbance. The professional community comprises a stew of conflicting approaches to mental and physical health, whose various proponents rarely talk openly with one another. There is a need for leadership from someone who could activate a unifying center. The idea of a new center also suggests that the focus wants to shift from the surface to the center of the whole person, from ego to Self.

Not long after I arrived in Seal Harbor, a dream gave me an image for the myth that almost fell on me:

"Waking early one morning, I see a large white parachute high in the air. It is illuminated by the first rays of the sun and descends very rapidly. I am awed and fascinated by its beauty and mystical power. At first it looks as though it will land some distance away, but as it gets closer to the ground it moves rapidly toward me until I'm afraid it will land on top of me. It stops short, however, and lands in a small tree. Now I see that it carries someone, a tall lean, fresh-faced figure of indeterminate age and sex. I think of it as a man, but he looks almost hermaphroditic. Carefully untwining his legs from the branches of the tree, he gives me a wonderful smile, and climbs agilely to the ground."

At the dawn of a new day, perhaps the very beginning of the Aquarian age, this personable, hermaphroditic being descends from the heavens and incarnates on earth. If he had landed on me, as he almost did, I imagine it would have been the end of me. My individual consciousness was endangered by the charismatic image of a New Age avatar—if not the savior himself, then his advocate. The fact that I had the dream and could reflect upon it saved me from megalomania, for it provided the opportunity to see this figure as the spiritual being he is, a god or a divine messenger who heralds the light of a new time. Had I identified with such godlike power, it might have required a severe breakdown to return me to myself.

The extreme form of identification with a myth is a kind of madness. However, lesser varieties of the failure to distinguish human from divine levels of reality are commonplace. A man looks at a woman and sees a goddess: virgin or whore, witch, mother or little girl, she who must be obeyed or destroyed. A woman looks at a man and sees warlock, wizard or guru, father, son or holy spirit, a knight in shining armor who will save her from herself, or a terrible Power preventing her life. Anticipating marriage or the move to a new city, a young couple expects to find Paradise. It is rare to perceive exactly what *is* in the world. Maybe we never do.

Just as universal images overlay the people, places, objects and events of the world around us, so also are components of our particular past experience superimposed upon present reality. Early childhood, long forgotten or dimly recalled, is especially potent in this respect, probably because mythic elements lend it weight. For instance, the woman who remembers childhood beatings or sexual abuse by her father carries myth as well as memory. The image of a father hurting his daughter has behind it the archetypes of an era in which brutal and rigid patriarchal patterns have damaged the vulnerable, childlike, feminine soul. Every man and woman bears the imprint of the myth, but only some have had the literal experience that determines its specific form.

The creative imagination, what Jung calls "the projection-making factor" in the psyche, spontaneously weaves the material of fantasy, dream and myth from a mix of past experience and archety-pal/spiritual reality. When it is not seen for what it is and given its proper place, such material intrudes upon daily life and creates a disparity between events and what they are perceived to be. If you doubt it, ask a husband and wife each to tell you about their breakfast conversation that morning. The discrepancies between their accounts will be of the same stuff as myth.

One part of the work of analysis is to sort past from present reality. Another is to distinguish the mythic life of the spirit from the outer world, and to give a place to each. Some people, lost in what I think of as the pink cloud view of spirituality, fail to honor the requirements of earthly life. Others, hopelessly entangled in a Sisyphian round of every day, are unaware of the spiritual factors that give life meaning. The right relationship between ordinary and non-ordinary realities requires a place to stand in the space between worlds. From such a vantage point we can see and honor the role of divine power in human affairs without claiming it as our own.

Three or four years after I became an analyst, I was asked to review four biographies of Jung that had been published almost simultaneously, a scant fifteen years after his death.[1] I took up the task naively, unaware of the challenge it would present, and soon became bogged down in what felt like quicksand. Something peculiar was happening in these books. If I had not known in advance that they were all about the same person I would never have guessed it from reading them. In spite of some common threads, they created four vastly different images of Jung.

At first I tried to be objective in order to discover who Jung really was. Then I realized it was impossible. I had come face to face with myth, and fragments of it danced in peripheral vision like fireflies in the night, distracting me from my path. Eventually I gave up all pre-

---

[1] The review, some parts of which are reproduced here, was published as "Looking for Jung: The Man in the Myth," in *Psychological Perspectives*, spring 1978.

tense of detachment and descended into the subjective matrix of the material. Only two things were clear. It is not easy to write about Jung, and it is equally hard to write about the brave souls who have ventured to record their observations, recollections and perceptions of the man.

I plunged into Marie-Louise von Franz's biography, *C.G. Jung: His Myth in Our Time*,[2] with pleasant anticipation. Von Franz has long been one of my favorite authors. In fact, she was once one of my mythic images, appearing in dreams and fantasies as a guiding spirit who embodied aspects of my then unconscious creative life. Her illumination of subjects ranging from fairy tales to active imagination, from myths of creation to the mystery of matter made manifest in number and time, has contributed decisively to my own relationship to Jung's work.

As I read this book, however, my enthusiasm flagged. My mind wandered, and only duty kept me going. When I leafed through it again recently, I found it hard to recapture the loss of spirit I experienced at the time, for it touches some of the most profound aspects of Jung's life and work. My difficulty came from something more mysterious than lack of interest in its content. I imagine it may have sprung from the collision of two myths. As if her own deft hand were covered by Jung's, von Franz's becomes heavy in this volume, her style hurried, her vitality damped. In his own writing Jung's spirit soars freely, as does von Franz's in her other work, but both are strangely muted here. It is as if the conjunction of two luminaries had blurred the individual light of each.

Although von Franz focuses on Jung's work, an image of the person is nonetheless apparent. Von Franz's Jung is a creative genius. He is forthright, a man of conviction who is inspired by the mystery of the Self and is unconcerned with ego power. Much of the time he is alone, pursuing his path with single-minded spiritual devotion, a latter-day Merlin whose creative daimon drives him to unearth the living spirit of modern man buried in the human psyche.

---

[2] Trans. Wm. Kennedy (London: Hodder and Stoughton, 1975).

Von Franz's image of Jung lies singularly close to my own image of von Franz. Who is it? Jung? Von Franz? My projection on both? Maybe it is something all three of us share. Perhaps it is myth.

Like von Franz, Laurens van der Post has been one of my heroes for many years. His gentle, poetic style warms and stirs me. He is a gentleman in the deepest sense of the word, while his love of the small and vulnerable, the feminine, and the bushmen of the Kalihari desert has endeared him to me. Nevertheless, I was sobered by my dawning recognition that to write about Jung is less than simple, and approached *Jung and the Story of Our Time*[3] with caution.

My uncertainty was well advised. The van der Post I thought I knew became as lost in his volume about Jung as "my" von Franz did in hers. Like von Franz's, van der Post's Jung is deeply committed to a spiritual task. His flavor, however, is different. This Jung has the quality of an English gentleman who is distinguished by his humility, reverence and devotion to the process of dreaming. He is honest to a fault and painstakingly careful in his work, overlooking no detail, however small. Van der Post's Jung is a wounded healer, a burdened man who is lonely and often filled with despair despite his endless capacity for childlike wonder. He is intimately related to the soul, emerging finally as a gallant knight errant courageously championing the cause of the rejected feminine in his quest to restore balance to human relationship.

It will come as no surprise that I would have described van der Post himself much as he describes Jung. Is the image man or myth?

I turned next to the work of Paul J. Stern. Because I had never heard of him, neither he nor his work offered a preexisting hook upon which to hang my mythology. I began to read *C.G. Jung: The Haunted Prophet*[4] with curiosity, and was soon engrossed in a drama I did not understand. The book's emotional overtones made me wonder what experience Stern could have had of Jung to motivate what sounds like a personal vendetta.

---

[3] New York: Pantheon, 1975.
[4] New York: Braziller, 1976.

Stern has spun a brisk and fascinating tale, but it is filled with ambiguity and innuendo. The Jung of whom he writes is a thoroughgoing scoundrel. Never before having heard Jung described in less than enthusiastic language, I read the book with wide eyes. Many of Stern's assertions seemed incredible to me, but I could neither verify nor deny them. Did Toni Wolff, Jung's mistress, *really* "demand forcefully and gauchely that Jung divorce Emma and marry her?" Are there *really* an unusually high number of suicides and other deaths among Jungian patients? Did Jung's famous belly laugh *really* sound like "neighing?"

The Jung that Stern describes is a pathetic creature at best, at worst an out-and-out son of a bitch. He is physically repulsive, cruel, self-serving and hungry for power, a megalomaniac who relentlessly seeks "enshrinement" as a prophet if not a god. He is consumed by fantasies of wealth and power and is notable for his "adroitness at extracting money from 'spirituality.'" Stern portrays an evasive, opportunistic thrill-seeker, a manipulator and user of people; a man who is disloyal to his superiors, emotionally constricted and in constant search of tricky shortcuts in his work with patients, preferring easy ways to the difficulty of careful analytic work. He teeters on the brink of madness and suffers from facile intellectualism, undertaking his psychological writing solely for the purpose of self-justification. Who is this Jung? Is he no more than an unconscious aspect of Paul J. Stern, or is he, too, a living piece of the Jungian myth?

Just as every human being casts a shadow, so does every god have a demonic side. If the demon is not linked to the god consciously, then it hides in the unconscious. The shadow side of godlike power in the hands of a Jungian analyst looks like the Jung of Stern's description, a horrifying specter of Jung's ideas when they are misunderstood or misused by naive, unethical or inflated persons. Patients often project the extraordinary healing power of work with the unconscious upon their analysts. The analyst who accepts this charismatic role, failing to see and refuse the temptation to play God, risks incarnating the healer archetype's Nazi-like, charlatan shadow. Paul J. Stern has revealed its ugly face.

I began the final volume of the four with as little preconception of its author as I had had of Stern. For all practical purposes, Barbara Hannah was unknown to me. After reading *C.G. Jung: His Life and Work,*[5] I regretted not having met her sooner. Perhaps I liked this book best because Hannah's Jung comes closest to expressing the fulness of my own myth. It seems more likely, however, that only her eighty-five-going-on-ninety years approximated the maturity prerequisite to tackling the overwhelming subject of Jung the man so close to his lifetime.

The Jung that Hannah describes is as distinct as each of the others. He is a patient man who struggles courageously with the large and small difficulties with which life confronts him. Because he finds it essential first to live one's mistakes and *then* to understand them, he lives deeply and fully, but feels that "the only unbearable torture is the torture of not understanding." Although every new challenge is hard for him, he takes them all seriously and shrinks from nothing. He is relentless in the painful and continuous process of facing himself, getting to know his deepest and most alien corners, seeking not ego knowledge but the infinitely larger thing that is *Self* knowledge. Hannah's Jung is a simple, natural, spontaneous human being who wants above all else to become whole.

What are these four images, created by four different authors from the same biographical facts? Where can Jung's true face be found?

It would be easy to say that the four Jungs belong to von Franz, van der Post, Stern and Hannah, each reflecting a piece of the biographer's psyche. No doubt it is part of the truth, but that explanation does not do justice to the phenomenon because it is too personal. It overlooks the autonomy of the myth-making function of the psyche, the "otherness" of the archetype that gives myth a degree of objectivity and independence of its carriers. For the same reason, it would miss the point merely to conclude that there are as many different images of Jung as there are individuals who have been touched by

---

[5] New York: Putnam, 1976.

him or his work. On one level that may also be true, but I want to venture a step further:

I would postulate that the image of Jung, as I have seen it in my own dreams and the dreams of many patients, as well as in these four books, is intimately related to individuation, the growth process that pushes the individual toward wholeness. "Jung" functions differently in the psyches of different people and within the same person at different stages of development. His image carries a process rather than a fixed set of ideas. I believe that one of the greatest gifts of Jung the human being was his extraordinary capacity to activate the potential for wholeness in each individual. In exploring the process of individuation, I think he has become the primary carrier of its mythic image.

Contemporary Jungians are in the position of the early alchemists, who projected the transformation processes of the psyche into chemical reactions. They did not choose to do so. It happened to them. If we project those same processes onto a man named Jung, it is not because we want to deify him. We can either find a relationship to the myth or turn our backs on it. It will have its effect in either case, but if we do not relate to it, we are likely to fall into one of two opposite traps: On the one side lies the temptation to identify with Jung's charismatic image, but on the other, we can flee so far from the living symbol that Jungian psychology loses touch with the spirit that gave it life and becomes a dead conceptual system.

If we are not conscious of its mythic aspect, Jungian psychology is likely to meet the fate of *late* alchemy whose symbolic and psychological meaning nearly became lost when the science of chemistry replaced the myth. To tap the meaning hidden in the myth, we have to separate it carefully from outer facts but not discard it. Then, in a hundred years or so, perhaps someone will be able to write an objective biography of Jung.

I learned about the paradoxical quality of Jung's image from a patient who had many powerful dreams of Jung. The fact that he had such dreams suggested to Peter and to the several analysts with whom he had worked that it was crucial for him to relate to the unconscious, but he bounced in and out of analysis like a rubber ball, never quite managing to connect with himself. Then he dreamed:

"I am in Dr. Jung's house, in his study. It is very quiet and peaceful. Jung sits in an armchair reading. I am seated on a footstool at his left. My head rests on his shoulder. We sit together like this for some time. After a while we go into the garden for a walk. We walk in a park in the shape of a square with a path running around its perimeter. When we have completed walking the entire path, Jung turns to me and says, 'Well, we must say good-by now.' I stretch up on tiptoes and kiss him on the left cheek. I begin to weep. He pats me kindly on the shoulder. I say, 'Yes, I must go to buy my shoes now.' I hate leaving him, but know that I must."

Taking the dream at face value, I expected Peter to leave analysis again at this moment, for Jung himself had said good-by to him. What happened was quite different, however. For the first time he was able to reflect upon himself and work actively on his dreams instead of being tossed passively back and forth by ambivalence.

The reason for the change lies beneath the dream's surface. Jung's garden belongs to Jung, not Peter. For Peter, it is a Paradise in which he is contained like a child. He does not exist in his own right, but rests in a state of eternal bliss as Jung's left-hand man. Then Jung takes him for a walk around the four sides of a park's perimeter. When it has been encompassed and bounded, a phase comes to an end and a new one must begin.

The square is an ancient symbol of the earth. Its four sides, which define the four directions of ordinary reality, contain the totality of existence in the world of every day. In walking around the square, Jung shows Peter that his identification with mythic wholeness must come to an end. In a manner of speaking, he has to leave his unconscious containment in Jung's womb and try to achieve his own wholeness in his own uniquely difficult personal life. Because it is Jung who does it, he can accept the pain of expulsion from the garden. He knows he must buy a pair of shoes, the hard-earned standpoint of personal consciousness that makes it possible to walk in the world. Only by leaving Jung, at Jung's own request, can the Jung in Peter become real. Thus does the image of Jung insist on individuation.

The story has another chapter. In due time Peter again fell under the spell of unconscious ambivalence. Although he did not stop coming to analysis altogether, he found reasons to miss two out of every three sessions for several months, stopped paying his bill and finally took a long vacation in Europe. When he returned he did not contact me for six weeks. Then he paid his bill, came to one session and missed the next two appointments. When I called to find out what had happened, a recording told me his telephone had been disconnected.

I lost patience and wrote Peter a brief, icy note that terminated our working relationship. He was hurt and angry, and wrote me a lengthy protest laced with provocative barbs. Telling myself that it was time for him to live in the real world and carry the consequences of his actions, I did not answer his letter. Later I recalled the dream in which Peter had kissed Jung good-by. Then I saw that when I refused to see him again I had unconsciously acted out Peter's dream Jung. I became a god and expelled Peter from Paradise. One way or another, the myth would have its way.

The protective embrace of a bigger-than-life figure can be dangerously seductive. Many years ago, I fell into the habit of using active imagination to ask advice of the Jung in me whenever I encountered a difficult problem. In time I grew dependent upon his canny responses and, like the lady from Zurich reputed to consult the I Ching before she knew whether to accept a dinner invitation, I went to Jung for every hangnail. The godlike figure of Jung made all the decisions while my consciousness became passive and lazy.

One day I approached Jung expecting him to pull me out of a depression. Suddenly he said, "I can't help you. Your only answer is your pain." I was stunned. When I did not move he flew into a rage and shouted, "Get out of here and live your life!"

I was badly shocked. For a long time I feared it meant that I would have to leave Jungian psychology altogether. Two years later I timidly ventured back for another discussion with him and he clarified his position.

"I didn't mean you should *never* come back. I only meant that there are some things you just have to live through. You were relying on me too much to pull you out of your messes."

Of course he was right. To touch such a profound source of inner wisdom entails a nearly irresistible temptation to overuse it. But if the Self remains projected onto another, the opportunity to become a whole human being is lost.

If we are lucky, when we identify with any image different from who we are, an inner compass will intervene to restore a truer course. Then identification with the gods can go only so far before it breaks down and breakdown returns us to ourselves. I find it fascinating and reassuring to realize that in some people, at least, the image of Jung serves that process. For its own fulfillment, the mythic figure of Jung seems to require its carriers to become conscious, optimally functioning human beings who live their own lives. Such a myth must indeed lie close to the heart of individuation.

10

When the Spirits Come Back

My last year in Los Angeles was a nightmare of growing disillusion with professional life. I cared about the psyche, about dreams, about people, but found myself increasingly enmeshed in status and power concerns that had nothing to do with my deeper interests. In fact, the more "successful" I became, the less able I felt to serve life or soul. I was burned out and confused, unable to separate myself from the exalted expectations that were thrust upon me by virtue of my position. More than once I dreamed that my environment was filled with poison. Soon after dreaming of a funeral at the Jung Institute, I decided to leave.

In the brooding woods and weather of the Pacific Northwest, my wounds began to heal. I put aside preconceptions about what my life should be and waited, listening for the inner and outer voices that would tell me what might be required of me next. I walked endlessly, reflecting about my dreams, thoughts, fantasies and feelings, paying careful attention to how I was moved to spend my time when I could do anything I chose.

It was not long before I began to experience the impact of what is buried in the earth of this country. Without knowing at first what affected me so deeply, I was touched by aspects of Native American tribal consciousness that appeared to seep through the soles of my feet. One day I "saw," behind the eyes of a psychologist friend, an immense Indian chief gazing at me with longing, yearning to be set free from his prison in an alien white body. The same week I noticed the designation "Redman's Cemetery" on a map and spent several days searching for an Indian burial ground, but only found traditional marble headstones with names like McGuire and Scott.

A visiting psychic said my house and the surrounding forest were swarming with Indians. A mediumistic friend dreamed that she met me on the street and saw earth on my face. I looked, she said, like an old Indian woman.

I remembered the dream a student had told me soon after he dropped out of the analyst training program several years earlier. He was working on an archaeological dig in his dream, apparently alone. At first he saw only fragments, a piece of bone here, a shard there. Gradually he became aware that others were digging too, in many different places not necessarily visible from where he stood. Finally he was shown the scope of the project. He and others were excavating the remains of an enormous animal that extended from one coast of North America to the other. Even then I had wondered if Native American consciousness could be the buried creature in his dream. Now I, too, was pulled into the task.

I began to learn what I could about the people who first occupied this land, spending long hours in anthropological museums and hiking for miles to experience the power spots people told me about when they learned of my interest. Meanwhile I read, finding out what I could about native life, legends, art and healing practices. I was struck by the respect for truth, for nature and for the heart in what I learned of tribal consciousness. In it I discovered a humility and capacity to live with other human beings that is profoundly lacking in the superimposed European culture, and a relationship to spiritual levels of the psyche that we have almost lost. I saw in native ways an integration of healing and art into life, a refusal to cut the living fabric that is woven simply and naturally into unified patterns.

Immersion in the land and the material it exposed me to took me inexorably deeper into mistrust of the profession that had contained me. My consciousness was too developed just to imitate Native American practices, but neither could I continue to ape the professional forms I had been taught. Six weeks after moving I resigned from the professional organizations to which I belonged. Two months later I had a terrifying dream:

"I awake knowing that in the night the Bomb has dropped. I am near the epicenter and am contaminated with radiation. A few people reach toward me, wanting to touch me. Most avoid me. If they touch me they will be irreversibly contaminated."

A day later the one strong professional connection I had maintained was unexpectedly and precipitously severed. Suddenly I found myself alone with an overpowering need to break old molds along with the terrible guilt this entailed. Seeking friends with whom I could talk about the psyche, I found more emotional support, psychological depth and good instincts among "ordinary people" with no psychological training than in many members of my profession. I learned to value the human condition in a new way. The exaggerated sense of specialness that adheres to professional practice began to fall away, and the depths of my own nature rose from the ashes of the life I had left behind.

Slowly absorbing my radioactivity, I reflected about the separation that exists between everyday life and the practice of analysis. Professional analysis carries the bias of the Judeo-Christian era, wherein a lot of attention has been paid to the tree of knowledge but the tree of life has all but disappeared. That is, the profession values knowledge, but does not always further the process of living. Sometimes life is "understood" out of existence before it has a chance to happen.

Many of the formal aspects of analysis protect analysts from certain hard things, but do not necessarily serve either patients or the psyche. Instead, they encourage an arrogance of professionalism that must be left behind if we are to mediate the psyche's healing capacities. Rooted in European tradition, psychoanalytic forms have a precarious existence on this soil in any case, unconnected as they are to the native psyche. The psyche behaves as if it wants to bridge the gap, not to regress to primitive methods but to decrease the disparity between analysis as it is practiced and life as it is on this continent.

Seeking to reduce that split in my own life, I began to experiment with conditions that would push the limits of traditional psychoanalytic models and integrate the work more deeply with the spirit of life and nature in the Pacific Northwest.

Then I met Sarah. It was my second September in Seal Harbor, just before the spirits came back.

Native people say they do practical things in spring and summer. They fish, gather berries and prepare to sustain themselves through the long dark winter. The spirits are away then, in the underworld, doing whatever they do there. In autumn, around the time of the equinox but not precisely then, they come back. Then the people go into their longhouses. They tell stories, dance spirit dances and gather songs and poems, living with the spirits all winter long while the bears hibernate.

When the spirits arrive in Seal Harbor you know it. The winds come and the tourists go home and the air is alive with *something*. When they came that fall I wanted to paint again. All the artists I knew said, "Don't take lessons, just paint," but I felt insecure and looked for a teacher. Someone told me Sarah gives a good class, and one day in September I telephoned her.

Something peculiar happened. After I identified myself and made my request, there was a long silence. Then Sarah began to talk. She talked for a long time. On the face of it she was explaining why she would not give another class, but I had the eerie feeling that she had found her way into my head. She spoke of what was on my mind, about an incompatibility between professionalism and life in the community.

As abruptly as she had begun talking she stopped. There was another silence. Then she asked, "Are you a *trained* Jungian analyst?" I assured her that I was.

"In that case," she said, "I might like to arrange a trade with you." I said, "Oh. Then let's meet and talk about it."

We did not talk about it. We made no formal arrangement. For almost four months we met at roughly two-week intervals and talked about whatever came up. Sometimes she came to my house, sometimes I went to hers. Occasionally her infant daughter was there, sometimes Sam, her husband. Sarah showed me slides of her work, critiqued mine, talked about the psychological significance of color. Gradually, in bits and pieces, she told me her story.

Before her move to Seal Harbor, Sarah lived near Mt. St. Helens. One day her inner world began to fall apart. Growing more and more disturbed as the days passed, she and the mountain erupted almost simultaneously. It was Helen's first eruption, Sarah's fourth. Against a backdrop of falling ash, gas-masked people and impassable roads, her friends tried to find help for Sarah while she felt herself splitting apart as she stood on the earth and tried to hold the moon in its orbit.

The discrepancy between the feminine spirit (moon) and the reality of Sarah's life as a woman (earth) was too great for her psyche to bear. Like so many women in our time, she tried to heal the split with her own body, forming a bridge between the earth and the Great Goddess of the moon, who has become autonomous and refuses to stay in her ancient orbit.

Eventually Sarah was hospitalized. In the hospital she felt invaded, depersonalized, denied permission to do the work she felt she must do, preventing the moon from crushing the earth while holding the feminine archetype in some semblance of connection to life. She mused, "If only my friends hadn't been so frightened. I was all right. I had to do what I was doing. I wish they could have just understood and supported me in it. Instead they distanced themselves and assumed that what I said had no significance."

She remembered one doctor who was kind to her and seemed to understand what was happening. Only one. When she saw a terrifying presence and asked him to do something about it, he knew enough to stand between her and it. She was grateful for the simple gesture that took her experience seriously.

"It happens every five years," she told me.

"When did you say was the last time?"

"1980."

It was not hard to figure out. Now almost thirty-nine, Sarah was approaching another break. When I asked if she thought that was so, she changed the subject.

Our next few meetings were punctuated by Sarah's more or less indirect questions, designed to discover my attitudes about psychosis and particularly about hospitalization. I told her that I had, on occasion, worked with psychotic episodes outside the hospital, when light medication could be arranged and a family member was willing to carry twenty-four-hour responsibility. Twice I had insisted on hospitalization. In both cases the men had guns and threatened to use them, one on himself, one on someone else.

Later she asked directly, "What would you do if I called on you the next time it happens to me?" I laughed. I did not know in advance. "I suppose," I said, "I would ask you what you were experiencing and take it from there." I showed her a book by John Perry[1] and told her of attitudes I share with him, that some psychoses constitute the psyche's attempt to heal itself; that hallucinations, delusions and so-called bizarre ideation are like dreams which, if properly understood and integrated, carry a process of development and healing rather than ultimate disintegration. I said that the shattering event called breakdown is often a dismemberment that helps us re-member who we were meant to be, and expressed the hope that if such a process could happen in the right way, it might not have to repeat itself.

The dynamic of psychosis manifests primitive levels of the psyche that polite contemporary society has all but buried. Specific content may be very modern, but the process, the pull to madness itself, is very old. It is the call to the spirit world that finds so little legitimate space in our materialistic culture. The psychotic's task is exactly the same as the analyst's, to connect this world with the other. The native mind knows enough to give special status to what ours labels psychosis. In it may lie the initiation of shaman and healer. It is a call to the healing of life itself, healing that begins as an involuntary descent into the place of the big dream.

Sarah and I had no contract, not even a verbal agreement, but I felt bound by my implicit promise to her. Five days after Christmas she paid me a visit. With her she brought an uncharacteristically decisive manner and a brown paper grocery bag filled with books. She emptied the books on the floor, sixteen novels by the same author. This man, she explained, had raped her when she was nineteen years old,

---

[1] *The Far Side of Madness* (Englewood Cliffs, NJ: Prentice-Hall, 1974).

and now she was going to turn him in. She had compiled a dossier on him from his writings.

Something about the way she spoke puzzled me. I remembered that she was first hospitalized at nineteen. Clearly she *had* been raped at that time, but was it a literal, outer-world rape or had something else happened to Sarah for which rape was an adequate symbol? I felt uncertain.

Suddenly, in mid-sentence, she put the books back into their bag, took a deep breath, leaned back and began to talk in a different way. Clearly and without pausing she told me first about her mother's murder, when Sarah was six, shot by a lover who then committed suicide. Next she described a series of difficult relationships with men, culminating in her first marriage. She had felt misunderstood, betrayed and abandoned each time, her inner experience and feelings rejected or ignored. Finally she told, in detail, about each of her four hospital experiences. Having finished her recital she stood up to leave. I observed that the rapist had taken many forms in her life. She nodded and left with her bag of books.

The following Saturday Sarah's husband Sam knocked on my door and asked if we could talk. He was troubled by the way Sarah had been acting, and wondered if she were on the edge of a breakdown. They were leaving that night for a ski trip at Mt. Rainier, and Sam hoped the wildness of the mountain would calm her. I agreed that it might, but felt uneasy and urged him to call if I were needed.

The next night the telephone rang. I talked with Sam, with Sarah, with Sam again. Then I wrote in my journal:

"Sarah Petrovici has crossed over. Sam called tonight, from a phone booth at Mt. Rainier, and told me Sarah is having a hard time. When I talked with her she said Sam's father was standing in the middle of the road with cars whizzing past, in terrible danger (a hallucination). I asked her what kind of a man he is, and she described *the most* wonderful, stable human being. I said, 'It must be terribly scary to have him in such danger.' She said yes. I asked if she wanted to come home. She said, 'definitely!' Sam wondered if it could wait until morning and she agreed. I asked if I could do anything more for her tonight. She said, 'Can you assure me safe passage? There have been a few problems.' I hesitated. How could I be sure? Then I said I thought I could. She sounded relieved. I will see her tomorrow."

That night I dreamed:

"I pass by David's office and stop in. There is a packed suitcase in the middle of the floor and the place is a mess. I realize that Sarah Petrovici went to see David professionally once or twice long ago, before I knew her, but she was dissatisfied. I leave his office and go to see Sarah. She is doing very well, almost fully recovered from her psychotic episode."

Sarah's appearance in my dream reveals and clarifies my inner connection with her. David is a well-known analyst who works in a traditional manner, but not too rigidly so. He appears to be bright, creative, competent and kind, a living image of the ideal psychotherapist. In the outer world Sarah had never seen him, but *I* had been his patient for a time and the Sarah within me had not been satisfied. Unrelieved light, beauty, order, truth, goodness, reason and moderation are not adequate to heal the primitive, creative woman.

In case I had forgotten, the dream reminded me that the traditional white, masculine analytical model can no longer carry the healing archetype for me, no matter how perfectly the work may be done, because it is too separated from the wounded one, too disidentified from the wildly irrational, creative, primitive psyche. The doctor-patient archetype has two poles that are bound together in the healthy person. The analyst who identifies too much with "doctor," forgetting that he is also "patient," fails to activate the self-healing power of the psyche in his outer-world patients because he unconsciously needs them to remain sick. The office of the traditional analyst is a mess, and is ready to be left.

Coming as it did at this moment, on the brink of Sarah's break, the dream gave me clear warning not to fall back into old professional ways. She would not find her sanity in "David's office." That the dream Sarah was doing very well also encouraged me to trust her outer-world counterpart's capacity to achieve safe passage.

Sam and Sarah did not reach home the next morning. Scenery whizzing past the moving car was more than Sarah could bear, and they stopped at a friend's house in the woods some distance from Seal Harbor. Responding to Sam's call I found my way there, knocked on the door and walked in, feeling a little like Goldilocks. Sarah lay on a couch with her eyes closed. I said, "Hi Sarah." Without opening her eyes she said firmly, "I will speak with no one but the Pope." And so it began.

Later that day Sarah pushed me away and ran about the room screaming, "Taboo, taboo, taboo! I am taboo! Don't touch me. I am contaminated." My dream of the Bomb came back to me. I said, "No. You are not taboo. I want to touch you. You don't have to carry it all by yourself." We worked on decontamination rituals repeatedly during the days that followed.

I did little to intervene in Sarah's healing process, beyond taking on some of her contamination and asking a helpful physician to prescribe very small doses of antipsychotic medication through the worst of the episode. That afternoon she was able to go home. I telephoned some friends and asked if they would help by being with Sarah a few hours each day. They, in turn, called people they knew. Before it was over, twenty-five community members in addition to her family had become involved. As long as it was necessary, Sarah had at least two people with her twenty-four hours a day. After five days she announced, "There is too much energy in this room. Some of you will have to leave." The "staff" was reduced accordingly. In a few more days she was able to manage her life again without a lot of extra help.

At the beginning, things happened too fast for me to give even brief instructions to the people who appeared at the door to be with Sarah. When there was a chance to communicate I said only a little: 1) Sarah is in an all-right space. Try not to be afraid of it. Fear is not good for her. 2) Be yourself as fully as you can. If you need to protect yourself, either physically or emotionally, do it. 3) Do whatever you can to understand what Sarah is trying to say and where she is at any given moment, without trying to change it. 4) Sarah's task is to build a bridge between this world and the world where she is. If you see any way to help her with that, do it.

Sarah's approval was required before anyone was permitted to spend time with her. She knew immediately who would be good for her, and most were a particular breed of cat. For the first time I became aware of specific qualities of the counterculture that came of age during the sixties. The Vietnam War, psychedelic drugs and the overriding chaos of that time left many human beings now in their thirties and forties deeply wounded. Some, of course, have covered up the damage and successfully identified with the cultural norms of their parents. Others are hopelessly lost. It is a third group of whom I speak. They have remained close to their wounds, without making woundedness a virtue, and are thereby blessed with singular compassion and a fundamental knowledge and trust of the primitive psyche lacking to most of us who are older. These were Sarah's companions through her most vulnerable time. Insofar as possible we protected her from people too unconscious of their own wounds, too identified with "health."

For my part, I struggled daily with the "David" in me, who dared not trust Sarah's process and wanted to yield to pressures to hospitalize her, to administer heavier doses of drugs, or to try in other ways to save her from her experience. At moments I was shocked and frightened by the extremes to which her psychosis took her. What if she hurt herself, or committed suicide, or had an accident, or never came out of it at all? In that small community, where everyone saw everything, I would surely have been burned as a witch!

This is the crux. There was never serious doubt about the best treatment for Sarah, but in choosing the best for her I put myself at risk. Those who know and can activate the healing power of nature touch ancient hatreds. Whiteman healing has for centuries flexed muscles of ego control, trying to subdue and dominate nature. Anyone who cooperates with nature in the native way stirs old fears, arousing the awful suspicion that nature remains bigger than we and will finally get us all.

Where there is death, however, there is also birth. Images of giving birth and of being born were daily events in Sarah's imagery. Many other themes recurred, including the search for her mother, interplanetary warfare, and the ever-present nuclear contamination.

One day she asked, a look of wonder on her face, "Did you know there are all these little fishes in the underworld?"

In touching Sarah we were all drawn into her inner space and were in turn connected to the deepest parts of ourselves, the stuff of mysticism, creativity and madness, all three. As the days passed I became aware that contamination by Sarah's process brought healing to everyone who participated, each in a different way. In addition, it contained the possibility for healing something larger than the sum of individuals, a malaise in the community among us. When a culture has, like ours, become so rational and "in control" that it is in fact insane, the totally natural and irrational may be our only sources of sanity.

One night Sarah took all the pictures in her house off the walls, "to avoid breakage," she said. At five-thirty the next morning an earthquake shook Seal Harbor. The earth stabilized only a little sooner than Sarah. Five days later she was able to come to my house for a therapy session, wearing a jaunty hat. With a mischievous smile she explained that it was her "halfway hat."

During that session she became quite agitated and revealed that a woman had refused to go on a trip with her and Sam because of Sarah's "mental condition." We talked about the fact that a lot of people feel that way. She had met such attitudes many times before, but the quality of her experience during this episode had left her open, unprepared to meet those who could relate to her only in socially negative terms. True to her new hat, our work was only half finished. Sarah had reconnected to herself, but she still needed to find her place in the community, to bring back the gifts she had found in another world and return them to life..

Colette, who had been with Sarah during the darkest nights of psychosis, suggested we all meet together. Not only Sarah, but all of us, needed a ritual in order to be comfortable with each other in the world of ordinary reality. A few days later Mary dreamed that we had a party to celebrate Sarah's successful passage.

Theoretically it sounded like a good idea, but when I imagined actually doing something of the sort I felt embarrassed. It was all very well to be so unconventional while Sarah was mad, but *now* ... ? The inner David threatened to engulf me. I struggled for several days before accepting that I had gone too far along my path to leave it now.

Meanwhile, Sarah made a blackberry pie and celebrated her mother's birthday for the first time ever. The following weekend Sarah, Sam, the baby and sixteen friends joined me in a ritual followed by a potluck dinner. Nick played Winter Wolf, a contemporary tribal drum, in the native heartbeat of the earth until everyone was seated. Then I put on a ceremonial robe and spoke:

"Colette imagined and Mary dreamed that we gathered together to make sacred the event in which we have all participated, to acknowledge and celebrate our mutual bond. We have come here today to do it. Sarah Petrovici crossed over into another world, the world of pure spirit. Now she has returned, successfully and safely, to the world of ordinary reality. She went to find the mother who was murdered when Sarah was a small child. She came back with a new name that was given her there, a secret name to hold in her heart. She came back with poems and with ideas for new paintings. She gave birth to herself and will be with us here in a new way, a part of this community as she has never been before.

"Sarah, we rejoice with you for your safe passage, and welcome you into your new life here. You made your journey for all of us, not for yourself alone, and each of us has been with you during a part of it. Recognizing the importance of what you have done for us, Rose has made you a pin, silver with lapis and a sliver of moonstone. Wear it proudly as a sign of your passage. Silver and moonstone hint at the feminine nature of your crossing. The circle of lapis signifies the enduring wholeness you can achieve if you complete your sacred task. For yourself, and for us, you have been called to build a bridge to the other world, a bridge of poems, paintings and tellings of what you have learned, what you have seen and experienced. You are asked to heal a painful separation between this world and the world of spirit. We share this profound wound with you. Almost all men and women in this culture participate in a split between everyday life and the life of the spirit.

"The traditions, even the language of Western medicine are harsh and unconnected to what we who are here today have experienced. Driven by fear and ignorance, traditional medicine and psychology call people like Sarah schizophrenic, crazy, insane, thereby justifying shutting them up in hospitals, cutting them and the rest of us off from the healing process that the psyche is trying to accomplish. Sarah pointed out to me the other day that schizophrenics don't get colds; and I told her about the fact that schizophrenics don't get cancer. Colds and cancer are the two primary diseases of this time and place. Both can be cured by schizophrenia! Think about that.

"The psyche knows how to heal itself. In passages like Sarah's, what we have to do is pay attention and take seriously the processes the psyche initiates, the language and images it gives us. Other times and places have been more connected to the spiritual realities that Sarah has experienced and the rest of us have experienced through her. Ancient religious mysteries, contemporary mysticism and so-called primitive people all know about death and rebirth, the dark night of the soul, transformation, vision quest, shamanic initiation. These are the ways, the languages and images of spiritual reality, that inform the psyche's self-healing.

"Sometimes a transformation process is long, slow and undramatic. Sarah's has been sudden and dramatic. Throughout her experience she spoke frequently in images of nuclear energy. It is as if a nuclear explosion took place in her psyche. We all felt the enormous amount of energy that was released, physical energy transformed abruptly into spiritual energy, body becoming psyche. We all worried about when Sarah—and therefore all of us—would begin to get some sleep. But so much energy had become available to her that she didn't need to sleep. Some of us heard Sarah say she had become contaminated by the radiation that had been released. Those of us who insisted on touching her anyway, who agreed to enter into this process with her, have in fact taken on some psychological radiation. We have experienced it in various ways, some positive, some negative.

"We all know that nuclear energy can be used either destructively or creatively. All of us here need to find creative and constructive use for what we have been through together so we will not be hurt by it. For better or worse, the Age of Aquarius is also the nuclear age, and we are the people who must find ways to live together and work together to carry the power of the psyche, the power of experiences like Sarah's, instead of washing our hands, isolating ourselves and sending our scapegoats out alone into the wilderness as generations before us have done.

"I have been deeply moved by the spirit of love and community that has come forth from all of you. Several of you have told me that your participation in Sarah's crossing has been extremely important. I'm going to stop talking now and hope that some of you will tell Sarah and the rest of us what the experience has meant to you."

Almost everyone spoke. Before we ate together, Sarah spoke too, and read a poem that came to her in the other world.

This was Sarah's story, but also my own. As I try to work in ways that touch tribal consciousness, I begin to experience the fabric of community revealed in the depths of the psyche. Threads were severed and the pattern badly obscured so long as I sat with patients only in my office, speaking to no one of what I saw there, cutting and labeling and handing down pronouncements ex cathedra, taking everything back to the ego as if there were no world out there, tearing the fabric so badly I missed it completely, missed my patients' lives and mine.

Native People know that in telling our personal stories we become connected to the larger tale the spirits are trying to bring into the world. Alone, each of us receives a small piece of the story, a piece essential to the whole. By telling, and listening, and putting together the fragments we hear, we get inklings of something larger. When we can live in conscious acceptance of the whole story, personal matters will find their proper perspective and we will be able to live with one another. Then I imagine analysts will be obsolete. We will all be able to activate the healing function in each other, as a natural and integral part of life.

But that is far in the future. Now it is February. Next month, around the time of the equinox, the spirits will go back to the underworld and the tourists return to Seal Harbor.

Studies in Jungian Psychology by Jungian Analysts

Limited Edition Paperbacks

Prices quoted are in U.S. dollars (except for Canadian orders)

1. The Secret Raven: Conflict and Transformation.
Daryl Sharp (Toronto). ISBN 0-919123-00-7. 128 pp. $13
A practical study of *puer* psychology, dream interpretation, mid-life crisis, the provisional life, the mother complex, anima and shadow. Illustrated.

2. The Psychological Meaning of Redemption Motifs in Fairytales.
Marie-Louise von Franz (Zurich). ISBN 0-919123-01-5. 128 pp. $13
Particularly helpful for its symbolic approach to the meaning of typical dream motifs (bathing, beating, clothes, animals, etc.).

3. On Divination and Synchronicity: The Psychology of Meaningful Chance.
Marie-Louise von Franz (Zurich). ISBN 0-919123-02-3. 128 pp. $13
Penetrating study of irrational methods of divining fate (I Ching, astrology, etc.), contrasting Western ideas with those of so-called primitives. Illustrated.

4. The Owl Was a Baker's Daughter: Obesity, Anorexia and the Repressed Feminine. Marion Woodman (Toronto). ISBN 0-919123-03-1. 144 pp. $14
A modern classic, with particular attention to the body as mirror of the psyche in eating disorders. Based on case studies, dreams and mythology. Illustrated.

5. Alchemy: An Introduction to the Symbolism and the Psychology.
Marie-Louise von Franz (Zurich). ISBN 0-919123-04-X. 288 pp. $18
Detailed guide to what the alchemists were really looking for. Invaluable for interpreting images and motifs in modern dreams. **84 illustrations.**

6. Descent to the Goddess: A Way of Initiation for Women.
Sylvia Brinton Perera (New York). ISBN 0-919123-05-8. 112 pp. $12
A timely and provocative study of the need for an inner, female authority in a masculine-oriented society. Rich in insights from analysis.

7. The Psyche as Sacrament: C.G. Jung and Paul Tillich.
John P. Dourley (Ottawa). ISBN 0-919123-06-6. 128 pp. $13
Comparative study from a dual perspective (author is Catholic priest and analyst), exploring the psychological meaning of God, Christ, the spirit, etc.

8. Border Crossings: Carlos Castaneda's Path of Knowledge.
Donald Lee Williams (Boulder). ISBN 0-919123-07-4. 160 pp. $14
The first thorough psychological examination of the Don Juan novels, bringing Castaneda's spiritual journey down to earth. Special attention to the feminine.

9. Narcissism and Character Transformation. The Psychology of Narcissistic Character Disorders. ISBN 0-919123-08-2. 192 pp. $15
Nathan Schwartz-Salant (New York).
A comprehensive study of the subject, drawing upon a variety of analytic points of view (Jung, Freud, Kohut, Klein, etc.). Theory and clinical material. Illus.

10. Rape and Ritual: A Psychological Study.
Bradley A. Te Paske (Minneapolis). ISBN 0-919123-09-0. 160 pp. $14
Incisive combination of theory, clinical material and mythology. Illustrated.

11. Alcoholism and Women: The Background and the Psychology.
Jan Bauer (Montreal). ISBN 0-919123-10-4. 144 pp. $14
Sociology, case material, dream analysis and archetypal patterns from mythology.

12. Addiction to Perfection: The Still Unravished Bride.
Marion Woodman (Toronto). ISBN 0-919123-11-2. 208 pp. $15
A powerful and authoritative look at the psychology of modern women. Examines
dreams, mythology, food rituals, body imagery, sexuality and creativity. Illustrated.

13. Jungian Dream Interpretation: A Handbook of Theory and Practice.
James A. Hall, M.D. (Dallas). ISBN 0-919123-12-0. 128 pp. $13
A practical guide, including common dream motifs and many clinical examples.

14. The Creation of Consciousness: Jung's Myth for Modern Man.
Edward F. Edinger, M.D. (Los Angeles). ISBN 0-919123-13-9. 128 pp. $13
Insightful study of the meaning and purpose of human life. Illustrated.

15. The Analytic Encounter: Transference and Human Relationship.
Mario Jacoby (Zurich). ISBN 0-919123-14-7. 128 pp. $13
Sensitive exploration of relationships based on mutual respect.

16. Change of Life: Psychological Study of Dreams and the Menopause.
Ann Mankowitz (Santa Fe). ISBN 0-919123-15-5. 128 pp. $13
A moving account of a menopausal woman's Jungian analysis.

17. The Illness That We Are: A Jungian Critique of Christianity.
John P. Dourley (Ottawa). ISBN 0-919123-16-3. 128 pp. $13
Radical study by Catholic priest and Jungian analyst.

18. Hags and Heroes: A Feminist Approach to Jungian Therapy with Couples.
Polly Young-Eisendrath (Philadelphia). ISBN 0-919123-17-1. 192 pp. $15
A highly original integration of feminist views with the concepts of Jung.

19. Cultural Attitudes in Psychological Perspective.
Joseph Henderson , M.D. (San Francisco). ISBN 0-919123-18-X. 128 pp. $13
Shows how a psychological attitude can give depth to one's world view. Illus.

20. The Vertical Labyrinth: Individuation in Jungian Psychology.
Aldo Carotenuto (Rome). ISBN 0-919123-19-8. 144 pp. $14
A guided journey through the world of psychic reality, including dreams.

21. The Pregnant Virgin: A Process of Psychological Transformation.
Marion Woodman (Toronto). ISBN 0-919123-20-1. 208 pp. $16
A celebration of the feminine, in both men and women. Explores the wisdom of
the body, eating disorders, relationships, dreams, addictions, etc. Illustrated.

22. Encounter with the Self: William Blake's *Illustrations of the Book of Job.*
Edward F. Edinger, M.D. (Los Angeles). ISBN 0-919123-21-X. 80 pp. $10
Penetrating commentary on the Job story, with Blake's original 22 engravings.

23. The Scapegoat Complex: Toward a Mythology of Shadow and Guilt.
Sylvia Brinton Perera (New York). ISBN 0-919123-22-8. 128 pp. $13
A hard-hitting study of scapegoat psychology in modern men and women.

24. The Bible and the Psyche: Individuation Symbolism in the Old Testament.
Edward F. Edinger (Los Angeles). ISBN 0-919123-23-6. 176 pp. $15
A major new work relating significant Biblical events to the psychological
movement toward wholeness that takes place in individuals.

25. The Spiral Way: A Woman's Healing Journey.
Aldo Carotenuto (Rome). ISBN 0-919123-24-4. 144 pp. $14
Detailed case history of a fifty-year-old woman's Jungian analysis, with particular attention to her dreams and the rediscovery of her enthusiasm for life.

26. The Jungian Experience: Analysis and Individuation.
James A. Hall, M.D. (Dallas). ISBN 0-919123-25-2. 176 pp. $15
The clinical application of Jungian thought, including details of the process of analysis, how and where to find an analyst, location of training centers, etc.

27. Phallos: Sacred Image of the Masculine.
Eugene Monick (Scranton/New York). ISBN 0-919123-26-0. 144 pp. $14
The essence of masculinity (as opposed to the patriarchy) through close examination of the physical, mythical and psychological aspects of phallos. **30 illustrations.**

28. The Christian Archetype: A Jungian Commentary on the Life of Christ.
Edward F. Edinger, M.D. (Los Angeles). ISBN 0-919123-27-9. 144 pp. $14
Psychological view of images and events central to the Christian myth, showing their symbolic meaning in terms of personal individuation. **31 illustrations.**

29. Love, Celibacy and the Inner Marriage.
John P. Dourley (Ottawa). ISBN 0-919123-28-7. 128 pp. $13
Explores the religious significance of Jung's work, showing how it challenges traditional theology and bridges the gap between psychology and religion.

30. Touching: Body Therapy and Depth Psychology.
Deldon Anne McNeely (Lynchburg, VA). ISBN 0-919123-29-5. 128 pp. $13
Illustrates how these two disciplines may be integrated in theory and practice. Deals with dance, the meaning of touch, dream interpretation and transference.

31. Personality Types: Jung's Model of Typology.
Daryl Sharp (Toronto). ISBN 0-919123-30-9. 128 pp. $13
Detailed explanation of Jung's model (basis for Myers-Briggs Type Indicator), illustrating its implications for psychological orientation and for relationships.

32. The Sacred Prostitute: Eternal Aspect of the Feminine.
Nancy Qualls-Corbett (Birmingham). ISBN 0-919123-31-7. 176 pp. $15
Shows how our vitality and capacity for joy depend on rediscovering the spiritual dimension of sexuality. Illustrated. (Foreword by Marion Woodman.)

33. When the Spirits Come Back.
Janet O. Dallett (Seal Harbor, WA). ISBN 0-919123-32-5. 160 pp. $14
An analyst examines herself, her profession and the limitations of prevailing attitudes toward mental disturbance, to rediscover the integrity of the healing process.

34. The Mother: Archetypal Image in Fairy Tales.
Sibylle Birkhäuser-Oeri (Zurich). ISBN 0-919123-33-3. 176 pp. $15
Illuminates the mother complex, with reference to positive and negative mother figures in many well-known fairy tales. (Edited by Marie-Louise von Franz.)

Prices and payment (check or money order) in U.S. dollars

Please add $1 per book (bookpost) or $3 per book (airmail)

INNER CITY BOOKS
Box 1271, Station Q, Toronto, Canada M4T 2P4